gENOCIDE
modern crimes against humanity

brendan january

twenty-first century books / minneapolis

photo acknowledgments

The images in this book are used with the permission of: © Brown Brothers, p. 13; © Armenian National Institute, Inc., courtesy of Sybil Stevens (daughter of Armin T. Wegner). Wegner Collection, Deutches Literaturarchiv, Marbach & United States Holocaust Memorial Museum., p. 16; © North Wind Picture Archives, p. 20; © Bettmann/CORBIS, pp. 24, 57, 63; © United States Holocaust Memorial Museum, p. 37; © AP/Wide World Photos, pp. 39, 67, 143; USHMM, courtesy of National Archives and Records Administration, College Park, p. 42; USHMM, courtesy of National Museum of American Jewish History, p. 46; © Michael St. Maur Sheil/CORBIS, p. 52; © AFP/Getty Images, p. 53; © H. Miller/Hulton Archive/ Getty Images, p. 54; © Claude Juvenal/AFP/Getty Images, p. 64; © Dudman Richard/CORBIS SYGMA, p. 69; © Wolfgang Kaehler/CORBIS, p. 72 (top); © Chris Rainier/CORBIS, p. 72 (bottom); © David Turnley/CORBIS, pp. 82, 84; © Carlo Allegri/Getty Images, p. 88; © Regis Martin/Getty Images, p. 95; © Patrick Robert/Sygma/CORBIS, p. 99; © Igor Dutina/AFP/Getty Images, p. 103; © Gilles Peress/ Magnum Photos, p. 105; © Fehim Demir/EPA/CORBIS, p. 107; © Langevin Jacques/CORBIS SYGMA, p. 113; © Espen Rasmussen/AFP/Getty Images, p. 121; © Sven Torfinn/Panos Pictures, pp. 123, 130; © Thomas Coex/AFP/Getty Images, p. 124; Courtesy of Dr. Jerry Ehrlich, pp. 126, 128 (both); © Photolure/Reuters/CORBIS, p. 134; © Joyce Naltchayan/AFP/Getty Images, p. 136; © Leonhard Foeger/Reuters/CORBIS, p. 138; © Damir Sagolj/Reuters/CORBIS, p. 140; © Howard Davies/CORBIS, p. 141. Maps by Laura Westlund, pp. 11, 44, 65, 78, 98, 120. Front Cover: © Paul Lowe/Panos Pictures (top); © Christophe Calais/In Visu/CORBIS (center). Back Cover: USHMM, courtesy of National Archives and Records Administration, College Park.

Twenty-First Century Books
A division of Lerner Publishing Group
241 First Avenue North
Minneapolis, Minnesota 55401 U.S.A.

Website address: www.lernerbooks.com

Library of Congress Cataloging-in-Publication Data

January, Brendan, 1972–
    Genocide : modern crimes against humanity / by Brendan January.
      p.   cm.
    Includes bibliographical references and index.
    ISBN-13: 978–0–7613–3421–7 (lib. bdg. : alk. paper)
    ISBN-10: 0–7613–3421–1 (lib. bdg. : alk. paper)
    1. Genocide—History—20th century. 2. Genocide—Case studies. I. Title.
HV6322.7.J36 2007
304.6'630904—dc22   2005032850

Manufactured in the United States of America
1 2 3 4 5 6 – BP – 12 11 10 09 08 07

contents

introduction
approaching genocide

This book recounts the most inhumane acts people have committed against their fellow human beings. It describes how individuals planned, organized, and built a vast machinery that had one purpose—the extermination of another group because of who it was. It tells of those who suffered, died, or resisted, and it discusses how one person summarized this process with a word that today represents history's greatest crimes—*genocide*.

In essence, genocide is murder. But more precisely, it is the result of a process that sets one group against another. This process has its roots in the way people see themselves and others.

"No man is an island," wrote English poet John Donne in the seventeenth century. Each individual is bound into a larger fabric of family, tribe, and nation. This is not always obvious to the individual—like a fish that never realizes it's in water. But many social interactions—the way individuals say hello, say good-bye, whom they care about and why, whom they fear, and whom they trust—is often dictated by an invisible web of social rules. These rules are necessary and typically beneficial, and they have existed since humans first came together to form societies. At their deepest level, the rules tell us who we are.

But this can have darker implications. A society can tell us who we are but also who we are not. In this sense, being part of a group means focusing on its differences from others: skin color, culture, history, religious or political beliefs, gender, or economic status.

Once again, this recognition of differences is natural and usually harmless. Sometimes, however, it becomes much more negative. Instead of just observing the differences in others, a group starts to label them as dirty, destructive, or evil. When this occurs, societies may organize to remove or segregate the differences. And in some cases, societies decide to get rid of those who are "different" altogether.

This book is about the process that is called genocide. Any description of genocide usually focuses on its extraordinary violence. However, history is filled with bloody battles, acts of cruelty, and broken promises. Armies have destroyed cities. Prisoners have been tortured and starved to death. Nations have bullied or cheated other nations. In each instance, innocent people were killed or mistreated. Even today, murder is common and stories about how one person took the life of another—often in an act of brutality—are regular features in the media. Why is genocide so different?

The crucial difference lies within the minds of those who commit genocide. They seek to destroy not just people—men, women, and children—but entire cultures. The perpetrators of genocide can do this by burning schools, libraries, and houses of worship; seizing homes and possessions; renaming streets; and paving over graveyards.

"Genocide is a crime on a different scale to all other crimes against humanity and implies an intention to completely exterminate the chosen group," wrote Alain Destexhe in *Rwanda and Genocide in the Twentieth Century*. "Genocide is therefore both the gravest and greatest of the crimes against humanity."

* * *

$f$ew words in our language seem to provoke the same furor, passion, and debate as *genocide*. It is used in mourning by survivors in annual ceremonies to commemorate their suffering. It is hurled at opposing groups during press conferences. It appears in books and newspapers regularly and is used in reference to subjects as diverse as abortion, discrimination, and animal rights. Academics and scholars argue endlessly over its precise definition.

Anyone who approaches the topic of genocide should be aware that determining the victims of genocide is a contentious and emotional issue today. The word has been used in connection with slavery in North and South America, the displacement of Native Americans, and Israeli policy and actions toward Palestinians. Genocide has also been used to describe famine in Ireland and Josef Stalin's rule in the Ukraine.

At their best, debates about genocide challenge conventional thinking, open history to different perspectives, and sharpen the meaning of words. They prevent any complacency and they maintain a focus on our capacity for inhumanity. However, these debates can also be unproductive. Saying that one group was a victim of genocide can be interpreted as a denial of another's suffering. At their worst, groups seem to jockey for a position on a kind of scale of victimhood. Politicians, concerned citizens, and scholars criticize one another for devoting too little or too much attention to any one group's experience.

Anyone who writes about genocide, regardless of his or her position, cannot avoid taking part in this debate. For example, simply including the Holocaust (the genocide against European Jews) alongside other genocides will be interpreted by some as an attempt to make the Holocaust appear to be less important— just another one of history's bloody events. Others may argue that additional groups suffered from genocide and that they should have been included or described in greater detail. No single exploration of this subject can address these concerns to everyone's satisfaction. The author encourages the reader to do more research on this subject, to seek out other opinions and views, and to arrive at his or her own conclusions.

This book is structured to describe the context and consequences of six genocides—the Armenians of the Ottoman Empire, the Jews of Europe, the Cambodians in the "killing fields," the Tutsis of Rwanda, the Muslims of Bosnia, and the Darfur tribes of Sudan. It also focuses on the efforts of a single individual to have the world recognize the monstrous crime genocide represents. All the genocides share common elements—the victim, the perpetrator, the rescuer, the survivor, and the witness. Whenever possible, the descriptions of genocide in this book are cited in the words of those who saw it firsthand.

However, no words or photographs can truly explain what happened or fully describe the impact genocide has on the individuals who experienced it. Dow Lewi, who was among the millions persecuted by the Nazis in World War II, wrote to his sister in Palestine shortly after the war ended. "I realize that you, over there, cannot imagine even a hundredth part of the suffering, fear, humiliation, and every kind of bullying that we lived through. People who live and think as normal people cannot possibly understand."

chapter one
the armenians of the Ottoman empire

$f$ew empires in history could rival the glory of the Ottoman Empire in the 1500s. After the conquests of Suleiman I (the Magnificent), the empire's territory stretched along the coast of North Africa, into southern Europe, and across the heart of the Middle East to the Persian Gulf. Its capital was Constantinople, an ancient city on the Bosporus Strait that stood as a gateway between Europe and Asia.

The Ottoman Turks ruled many peoples, each with its own culture. The Ottoman Turks were Muslims who practiced the religion of Islam. Jews and Christians were allowed to practice their faith and customs, since Islam acknowledged its roots in those two religions. However, many Muslims regarded these groups with suspicion because they had never converted to Islam, and non-Muslims often didn't have the same rights or privileges Muslims enjoyed.

One of the subject peoples in the Ottoman Empire were the Armenians, a Christian group. For one thousand years, the Armenians had lived in the rugged mountain region of central Asia—now in eastern Turkey. The harsh landscape and long winters helped insulate the Armenians from outside invaders. Although they were ruled by the Ottoman Turks, they kept their language, culture, and identity intact.

Over time, the Armenians prospered. A middle class emerged, and Armenians took on important positions in

This map of Europe shows the territory of the Ottoman Empire during the 1500s.

commerce and trade. Though officially second-class citizens, the Armenians became envied by other Turks and distrusted by those in the Ottoman government, who were uneasy because the Armenians held so much power in the empire.

This unease grew as the Ottoman Empire went into decline. Leadership of the empire was often contested with violence. Former areas of the empire—such as Greece and large areas of the Balkans—won their independence. Enemies, sensing the empire's weakness, struck at its borders. By 1834 Russia was pushing hard from the northeast, and France invaded Algeria, a region ruled by the Ottomans in North Africa.

The rulers of the Ottoman Empire were shaken by these events. In the 1500s, the Ottoman armies had threatened Europe. Now the situation was reversed. Everywhere, it seemed, non-Turkish, non-Muslim people were rising up to challenge Ottoman rule and authority. As the Armenians grew stronger, they also began to agitate for reform. They resented that one man—the sultan—ruled their affairs. They didn't like their second-class status within the empire. They were also angered that other groups in the empire, such as the Kurds, attacked them and seized animals and crops for bribes, while the Ottoman authorities did nothing.

To the Ottoman Turks, the Armenian challenge was a serious one. The Armenians lived in the eastern half of what the Ottoman Turks regarded as their homeland. Turks had displaced Armenians and lived among them for generations. To grant the Armenians any power over their affairs was humiliating enough; to give them territory for their own state was unthinkable. Consequently, the Ottoman Turks conceded nothing to the Armenians. In response, the Armenians grew more restless and their demands became louder. And with each new sign of Armenian power and independence, the Ottoman Turks grew more fearful, angry, and determined to solve the "Armenian Question." The late 1800s and early 1900s were rocked by revolts and sudden spasms of large-scale violence against the Armenians. In 1892 Turkish forces crushed an Armenian rebellion in the Sassun region. Turkish leaders believed large portions of the Armenian population actively supported the rebels, so the Turks continued their attacks. By 1896 it is estimated that between 200,000 and 300,000 Armenians had beeen killed.

In the early 1900s, there was a moment of hope when a group of leaders called the Young Turks seized power. The Young Turks were determined to reform the empire, and at first it seemed that they would reach out to the empire's minorities. One of the Young Turks, Ismail Enver, declared, "Henceforth we are all brothers. There are no longer Bulgars, Greeks, Romanians, Jews, Muslims. Under the same blue sky we are all equal, we glory in being Ottomans." But soon the Young Turks took on the same views as the sultan they had replaced. Minorities such as the Armenians were seen as enemies from within, sucking the energy and strength from the empire.

Moreover, the Ottoman Turks were deeply concerned that the Armenians occupied important positions, which made Armenian demands for independence appear much more sinister. The Armenians also guarded their culture through their tight-knit communities and network of schools. They were Christians who had never accepted Islam, and so, to the Ottoman Turks, they seemed to be rejecting their rule and culture. For the Young Turks, the Armenian Question took on darker and darker implications. Only when the treacherous

A unit of the Young Turks march through the streets of Constantinople after overthrowing the Ottoman government in 1908.

elements were removed from within could they face their enemies beyond the borders.

In 1914 the world was engulfed by war. The spark that began the conflict occurred in July, when a young Serbian shot the crown prince of Austria-Hungary and his wife as they were riding in an open car through the streets of Sarajevo. Both were killed instantly. The incident ignited World War I, one of the worst wars in history. Austria-Hungary attacked Serbia. In defense of Serbia, Russia threatened Austria-Hungary. Germany came to the aid of Austria-Hungary by warning Russia to back down. France, bound by alliance with Russia, threatened Germany. Orders were sent to army units and everywhere young men scrambled to gather their weapons, uniforms, and equipment. Frantic telegrams were exchanged between the nation's leaders, pleading for peace or blustering about war. Finally, German armies marched into Belgium to begin the invasion of France. Great Britain promptly came to the aid of France. Across Europe, the roads were choked full of marching soldiers, all headed to battle.

For the Ottoman Turks, the war was seen as a challenge and an enormous opportunity, and the Ottoman Empire joined the war on the side of Germany. The Ottoman Empire was now fighting for its very survival, and the Young Turks had a window of opportunity to do what they wished without foreign influence. The Armenians, already in a precarious position within the empire, soon found themselves regarded as part of the enemy. Many Armenians lived across the Ottoman border in Russia, and tens of thousands of them enlisted in the Russian army, a fact that Turks would later cite to justify their view that the Armenians were a mortal enemy who had to be destroyed.

Ismail Enver, who had earlier said ". . . we are all brothers," had become the minister of war. He led a 100,000-man army to attack Russia and slice through to India, where he believed he would be greeted as a liberator and establish the foundation for an empire of Turkic-speaking peoples. However, Enver's men were ill equipped for the bitter winter. Trapped on icy paths and struggling through snowdrifts in the mountains, thousands died from exposure. When the ill-conceived offensive ground to a halt, Enver had only 10,000 men left, and his forces had achieved nothing of significance.

Answering the Armenian Question

Against the backdrop of this disaster, the Armenian Question took on new urgency. The Ottoman Turks believed the Armenians would help the Russian army invade. Dr. Nazim, a high-ranking Turkish official, told a group of leading Ottoman Turks that even one Armenian still in the empire represented a dire threat. A series of orders came out of Constantinople that said the Armenian people were to be resettled. The process started in early 1915.

"Word came that they were going to transfer us," recalled Takouhi Levonian, a fourteen-year-old Armenian at the time. "Every household began preparing by making kete [an Armenian bread], preparing chickens, other meats, and so on. My father told my mom not to bother with any of these preparations. He said to just take our bedding on the mules and not to bother burying anything, like so many others had done who thought they would return to them. He said that if we ever returned, he would be glad to come back to four walls. He was farsighted."

In many instances, the Ottoman Turks summoned the men separately or by official notice. They were told that they were to be resettled and that the government did not intend to harm them. Once the men had reported, they were marched out of the village to a remote place and murdered.

In other cases, the men were told to report with their families for resettlement. Once again, they were not told where they were actually going. "We were the first caravan to leave with much tears and anguish since it meant separation for so many," said Levonian. "They assigned a few soldiers to us and thus we began. We used to travel by day, and in the evening we stopped to eat and rest. In five to six days we reached Palu. There while we were washing up, I will never, never forget, they took my father away, along with all the men down to twelve years of age."

With the men out of the way, the authorities kept the caravans on the march for days, mostly into barren or empty

Two Armenian boys with bare and bandaged feet starved to death during a caravan through the desert.

desert regions, where the people were forced at bayonet point to keep walking without food or water. Those who did not die from exposure fell victim to starvation. Many Armenian parents, frantic and desperate, gave their children to Turkish and Kurdish families, who raised them and converted them to Islam.

Morgenthau's Plea

The American ambassador in Constantinople, Henry Morgenthau Sr., began to hear stories about Armenians that seemed too horrible to believe. He then met survivors themselves and received letters from witnesses in the countryside. In June 1915, Morgenthau wrote to his superiors in Washington, D.C., saying that the deportations "represented a new method of massacre. When the Turkish authorities gave the orders for these deportations, they were merely giving the death warrant to a whole race; they understood this well, and, in their conversations with me, they made no particular attempt to conceal the fact."

Morgenthau said the caravans could be seen "winding in and out of every valley and climbing up the sides of nearly every mountain—moving on and on, [those deported] scarcely knew whither, except that every road led to death."

> In a few days, what had been a procession of normal human beings became a stumbling horde of dust-covered skeletons, ravenously looking for scraps of food, eating any offal that came their way, crazed by the hideous sights that filled every hour of their existence, sick with all the diseases that accompany such hardships and privations, but still prodded on and on by the whips and clubs and bayonets of their executioners.

And thus, as the exiles moved, they left behind them another caravan—that of dead and unburied bodies, of old men and women dying the last stages of typhus, dysentery, and cholera, of little children lying on their backs and setting up their last piteous wails for food and water. There were women who held up their babies to strangers, begging them to take them and save them from their tormentors.

Morgenthau expressed his fury directly to the Turkish government in his meetings with an official, Mehmet Talaat. During one, Morgenthau brought up eyewitnesses to the slaughter, but Talaat grew irritated.

"Why are you so interested in the Armenians anyway?" he asked. "You are a Jew, these people are Christians. . . . What have you to complain of? Why can't you let us do with these Christians as we please?"

"You don't seem to realize that I am not here as a Jew but as the American Ambassador," answered Morgenthau. "I do not appeal to you in the name of any race or religion but merely as a human being."

Talaat seemed unable to grasp Morgenthau's point. "We treat the Americans all right, too," he told the ambassador. "I don't see why you should complain."

By the time Morgenthau had spoken to Talaat, other governments had already acted. On May 24, 1915, France and Great Britain issued a declaration saying that the massacres were "crimes committed by Turkey" and that France and Great Britain would "hold all members of the Ottoman Government, as well as such of their agents as are implicated, personally responsible for such massacres."

The Armenians received similar messages of support throughout the war. In France Premier Aristide Briand stated,

"When the hour for legitimate reparation shall have struck, France will not forget the terrible trials of the Armenians."

However, little was done (or could be done) on the ground. In early 1916, Morgenthau left Constantinople. "My failure to stop the destruction of the Armenians," he later wrote, "had made Turkey for me a place of horror—I had reached the end of my resources."

First Reactions to the Genocide

World War I raged for four years, costing millions of lives and leading to the destruction of the German, Austrian, Russian, and Ottoman empires. The Ottoman Turks, having fought on the side of the Germans, were among the defeated when the war ended in November 1918. New representatives were appointed to the Turkish government to negotiate with the Allies. Many of the Young Turks boarded a ship and fled the country to find refuge in Germany.

The new Turkish government was aware of the slaughter of the Armenians, and some high officials began an investigation to find the guilty and bring them to justice. The British and French occupiers also initiated an investigation to settle several issues, including what had happened to the Armenians. These efforts, however, largely failed. The British and French soon became distracted by other issues, and the Turks, though defeated, grew more resistant. The British prosecution bogged down over the question of twenty-nine British prisoners held by the Turks, who offered to swap them for more than one hundred Turks held by the British. Many of these prisoners had been accused of taking a role in the genocide. Eventually, the British grew more concerned about their soldiers and less about the Armenian Question, and the trade was completed.

Talaat, who had settled in Germany, blamed the murders on "uncontrolled elements"—soldiers who had disobeyed orders and acted more cruelly than necessary. "Innocent people," he admitted, "were molested," but this "regrettable" fact was due to the pressures of the war and because of the Armenians themselves, he wrote. Other countries, he argued, also committed crimes during the war, but these were overlooked, while in Turkey, "everybody's eyes were upon us."

Despite these claims, the trial in Turkey proceeded. Seven of the leading perpetrators were tried, found guilty, and sentenced to death. But by then, these individuals had fled Turkey, and not one of the sentences was carried out. In Turkey the new government was determined to forge a new country out of the

Large numbers of Armenians were buried in mass graves after the massacres ended in 1918.

remains of the Ottoman Empire. In their eyes, there was no point in dwelling on what had happened to the Armenians.

By this time, the Armenian population in the Ottoman Empire had been decimated. Of the nearly 2 million Armenians who were alive at the start of the war, 1 million had died in the genocide. About 250,000 had escaped, another 200,000 had been forced to convert to Islam, and about 400,000 somehow survived.

Most of the surviving Armenians in what was now Turkey, as well as Armenian communities around the world, were too focused on survival to do much immediately after the genocide. Some, however, were angered that justice had been frustrated.

chapter two
crusader raphael lemkin

mehmet Talaat lived comfortably as an exile in Germany. Germany had already refused Allied demands for him to be tried for his crimes, and as time passed, other problems appeared more pressing than justice for the massacres in Turkey. It appeared that Talaat would be able to live the rest of his life without facing responsibility for what had happened. However, on March 14, 1921, a young man crept behind Talaat as he strolled near his Berlin home. The man thrust a pistol at the back of Talaat's head and screamed, "This is to avenge the death of my family!" The sound of the shot exploded through the neighborhood, and Talaat fell to the ground. The young man was hauled to the local police station, where he was charged with murder. His name was Soghomon Tehlirian, a twenty-one-year-old Armenian. He explained that his mother, three sisters, and two brothers had been killed in Turkey and that his act was not a matter that should concern the Germans.

Tehlirian's actions made international news. In Poland a twenty-one-year-old Jew named Raphael Lemkin spotted the story in a local newspaper. Lemkin asked one of his professors why the Armenians didn't simply have Talaat arrested for the massacres and put on trial.

There is no law that allows it, was the reply. The professor elaborated. "Consider the case of the farmer who owns a flock of chickens. He kills them and this is his business. If you interfere, you are trespassing."

The answer made little sense to Lemkin. Tehlirian was charged with the crime of murdering one man. Talaat, however, who was responsible for the murder of more than one million people, faced no charges. "A nation was killed and the guilty persons were set free," Lemkin later recalled. "Why is a man punished when he kills another man? Why is the killing of a million a lesser crime than the killing of a single individual?" And, he reasoned, the Armenians weren't "chickens" owned by the Turks to do with as they wished.

This was not the first time Lemkin had shown interest on the subject of how people could commit mass murder. As a boy, he was fascinated by stories of the Roman Empire, especially of its emperor Nero, who threw Christians to lions in a bid to wipe out the new religion. Lemkin peppered his mother with questions. How could such a thing happen? Why would people allow it? How could they cheer these bloody acts?

Raphael Lemkin worked tirelessly during his lifespan to come up with a plan for the prevention and punishment of genocide.

Lemkin had more to ponder, this time closer to home. In his area of Poland, then ruled by Russia, mobs attacked Jews, murdering some and beating others severely. Lemkin remembered the stories of the Christians murdered in ancient Rome. He saw a connection linking the two.

Later, as a law student at Lviv, Lemkin scanned through books of law codes from modern and ancient civilizations. He searched for some law that prohibited the slaughter of one group by another. The search proved fruitless, and so in the late 1920s, he began to write his own. In 1933 Lemkin presented a draft of this law to an international conference in Madrid, Spain.

Lemkin's law had two primary purposes. The first was to make it illegal for one group to murder another group based on religion, nation, race, or any kind of social distinction. The second purpose was cultural. A people could be murdered, said Lemkin, but their culture could also be destroyed through vandalism, theft, and destruction. In some ways, this could be considered just as profound as the act of murder. Lemkin called for other nations to intervene when such actions, which he labeled "barbarity," took place.

The reception to Lemkin's draft was not positive. Europe was a divided continent in the 1930s. The nations' economies were fragile, and the memories of World War I were still fresh and bitter. Some people questioned why Europeans should care about something that had happened in Turkey a generation ago. Others refused to endorse the idea that one nation could intervene in another's business. As Lemkin's draft was read, the president of the Supreme Court of Germany walked out in protest. While Lemkin's proposal was not openly rejected, it was referred to a committee and was not formally discussed again. Lemkin was deeply disappointed. "Cold water was poured on me," he later said.

When Was the First Genocide?

Raphael Lemkin asked an important question: have people killed entire groups throughout history? In the third century B.C., a Greek writer named Dicaearchus noted in a work entitled *On the Destruction of Human Life* that some people have died because of the destruction of an entire group. Many seminal texts, including the *Iliad* and the Bible, have references that include the slaughter of an entire people—men, women, and children. Some historians have argued that this should not be taken literally and that archaeological excavations do not reveal burned cities and signs of massacre. However, there are many historical examples of Greek city-states crushing their neighbors in what historian Peter Green called "the habit of genocide." Historian Bill Leadbetter cited another example of a Greek city-state that destroyed a rival four times and killed or enslaved every inhabitant. "Is this genocide?" he asked. "It certainly looks a great deal like it." Leadbetter concluded, "Modernity may have brought genocide to new ideologies and technologies, but the phenomenon may well be as old as civilization itself."

The Threatening Storm

Lemkin continued to address law gatherings with more and more urgency as global events were taking a grim turn. The world had fallen into an economic depression. In Germany a World War I veteran named Adolf Hitler had exploited economic problems to seize power as the head of the Nazi

Party. Hitler believed the German people had been undermined and weakened by the Jews, whom he claimed were directly responsible for Germany's defeat in World War I.

In 1931 Hitler had given an interview with a German newspaper editor. In it he spoke of establishing a German empire in eastern Europe where millions of people would be moved and millions killed. "We intend to introduce a great resettlement policy; we do not wish to go on treading on each other's toes in Germany. Think of the biblical deportations and the massacres of the Middle Ages. And remember the extermination of the Armenians. One eventually reaches the conclusion that masses of men are mere biological clay."

On September 1, 1939, German armies invaded Poland. Days later, Great Britain and France declared war against Germany, and World War II began. As the German soldiers and tanks swept over the landscape, Lemkin and thousands of other Poles fled. While Poland bitterly resisted the German onslaught, it could not recover when the Soviet Union, according to an earlier deal between Hitler and the Soviet dictator Josef Stalin, attacked Poland from the other side. Caught between these giant enemies, Poland was crushed and divided between the two powers.

Lemkin ended up in the part of the country ruled by the Soviet Union. Sensing that the world was entering a new era of horror and evil, he fled to the United States. He believed that such a powerful country could prevent what he feared was about to happen—the massacre of European Jews.

"A Crime Without a Name"

Lemkin secured a teaching position at Duke University in North Carolina and arrived in the United States in April 1941. As soon as he was settled, Lemkin tried to spread word of what was happening in Europe. Rumors were already spreading of mass executions, of resettlements, and of camps where unbelievable things were happening. Lemkin spoke to any group who would listen to him. He addressed political leaders, urging them to make some kind of gesture or declaration.

But even after the United States entered World War II in December 1941, Lemkin grew disappointed that his message was not being heard. One of the problems, Lemkin realized, is that he didn't have a specific word for what he was describing. The German Nazis were waging a brutal war against Jews. All Jews—men, women, and children—were targeted. Jewish culture and history in eastern Europe were also being destroyed.

In Lublin, Poland, Nazi soldiers ransacked the library at the Jewish Theological Seminary. They piled the books on a massive pyre in the market square and set it aflame. Lemkin believed this act, in its own way, was as destructive to the Jewish culture as murder. The books contained centuries-old thoughts, a collection of knowledge that enriched all peoples. Now all of it had been reduced to ashes. And no group's identity, said Lemkin, could survive without a past.

Of course, the annihilation of Jewish identity is exactly what the Nazis intended, and they followed a similar pattern of destruction throughout Europe, especially in the east. In some areas, they stripped Jewish cemeteries of their headstones. The Nazis were literally erasing the Jewish people from the landscape and from history. In a century, they cheerfully assumed, travelers would journey through regions and never know that the Jews had once existed there.

In a speech, the British prime minister, Winston Churchill, described the Nazis' actions as a "crime without a name." Churchill's phrase stuck with Lemkin. The problem, Lemkin reasoned, was that people couldn't recognize or understand what was happening because there was no word to explain it.

"Genocide"

Lemkin decided to come up with his own word. As an attorney, Lemkin was trained to take words and their gradations of meaning very seriously. But how could he come up with one word or phrase to describe what was happening in Europe? Mass murder didn't capture how the Nazis were trying to wipe out Jewish history and culture. Another option he considered, *Germanization*, didn't account for how the Nazis were physically killing all Jews. In any case, the word also failed to be universal—Lemkin wanted to describe a process, not just what was happening in Europe to the Jews at that time.

Lemkin was also very practical. He wanted a word that would be distinct and carry moral authority. When people used this word, it should mean something and never be confused for anything else. In this Lemkin took some inspiration from George Eastman, who had founded and named the Kodak camera company. Eastman said he had picked the word Kodak because it was short, was easy to say, and would never be confused for anything else. After much thought, Lemkin took the Greek prefix, *genos*, meaning "tribe, group, or nation," and combined it with the Latin word *cidium*, which means "to kill." Lemkin had created the word *genocide*.

Lemkin described genocide as a "coordinated plan of different actions aiming at the destruction of essential foundations of the life of national groups, with the aim of annihilating the groups themselves." In other words, genocide was a kind of assault on a culture through various means. It could be by killing people, but it could also be by forbidding the use of a language or by the destruction of a culture's monuments. "It became clear to me that the diversity of nations, religious groups and races is essential to civilization because every one of those groups has a mission to fulfill and contribution to make in terms of culture," Lemkin later wrote.

Lemkin continued to lobby U.S. politicians to do something about what was happening in Europe. He urged them to declare publicly that the protection of Jews and other minorities was a war priority. President Roosevelt sent a note to Lemkin, assuring him that some action would be taken but that he should be patient. "'Patience' is a good word to be used when one expects an appointment, a budgetary allocation, or the building of a road," Lemkin later wrote. "But when the rope is already around the neck of the victim and strangulation is imminent, isn't the word 'patience' an insult to reason and nature?"

Another part of the problem, Lemkin discovered, was that the reports coming out of Europe were simply unbelievable. Dark stories of execution squads, of disease-ridden ghettos filled with starving Jews, and of death camps where thousands of people were exterminated in gas chambers continued to circulate.

The people hearing these reports found them incomprehensible. Many dismissed them as rumors; others thought that the Allies were doing all they could to crush Nazi Germany. Lemkin despaired. A fellow Pole killed himself in London, leaving a note that said in part: "The responsibility for this crime of murdering the entire Jewish population of Poland falls in the first instance on the perpetrators, but indirectly also it weights on the whole of humanity, the peoples and governments of the Allied States, which so far have made no effort toward a concrete action for the purpose of curtailing this crime."

chapter three
the jews of europe

the genocide of European Jews was possible because of anti-Semitism that reached back hundreds, even thousands, of years. To the common people of medieval Europe, Jews were objects of suspicion, fear, and contempt. Jews, they thought, used the blood of Christian children in barbaric rituals. Jews were considered diabolical, secretive, sneaky, and dirty. Any calamity or misfortune that befell a community—a sick child, a failed crop, a tin of spoiled milk, or dead farm animals—was believed to be the work of Jews. "What then shall we Christians do with this damned, rejected race of Jews?" asked the German priest and revolutionary Martin Luther in 1543. "Since they live among us and we know about their lying and blasphemy and cursing, we cannot tolerate them."

Luther urged the "setting of fire to their synagogues and schools and covering over what will not burn with earth so that no man will ever see a stone or cinder of them again." In the German city of Bamberg, Jews were forced to wear a yellow patch or a peaked hat so they could be more easily identified.

Das Volk

German anti-Semitism was the product of centuries of belief, thought, and attitudes. The Germans were a people long before they were a nation. The German word for people is *das Volk* (the equivalent in English is "folk"). Das Volk was bound together by history, culture, and language. It was not created by national borders on a map. The Germans saw themselves as members of a common race.

This attitude may be difficult for a modern young person to understand. In countries such as the United States and Canada, immigrants can become citizens by fulfilling requirements and passing some tests. Moreover, anyone born within U.S. borders is legally considered a U.S. citizen. Immigrants, of course, can face discrimination or not be accepted by other Americans, but they ultimately are still members of the same country.

In contrast, Germans identified themselves as Germans because of their bloodlines. Jews and Germans lived side by side in the same towns for centuries. Jews spoke German as their first language, made significant contributions to German art, literature, and thought—and yet many Germans could not regard the Jews as Germans. Germans identified the Jews as members of a different race. Jews were not part of das Volk.

German anti-Semitism relaxed somewhat in the late 1700s and 1800s. Then in 1873, the stock markets plunged and many Germans lost their savings. In rage, they blamed a Jewish conspiracy for the disaster, using centuries-old stereotypes of Jewish bankers and speculators. Anti-Semitic writing and thought revived throughout Germany. Pamphlets and books blamed the Jews, declaring that they wanted to destroy the new German nation. One publication, *The Victory of Jewry over Germanness*, went through twelve printings between 1873 and 1879.

"The Jews," writes historian Gordon Craig, "were described as being by their very nature an alien element in German society, as being carriers of a disease that contaminated its vital forces and threatened it with degeneracy and death." This general hatred of Jews—combined with extraordinary historical circumstances and a single individual—would culminate in what many people today consider to be the greatest crime in history.

Adolf Hitler

Adolf Hitler was born in a small Austrian village just across the border from Germany in 1889. As a teenager, Adolf became interested in German nationalism, or the idea that all Germans should be in one country. At that time, Austria was part of the Hapsburg Empire. The empire's capital city was Vienna, and it counted numerous peoples as its subjects, not all of whom were German. The empire, with its polyglot of races and languages, disgusted Adolf.

As a young man, Adolf settled in Vienna, where he hoped to study art. In this city, Hitler later claimed, he learned to passionately hate Jews. In Hitler's mind, Jews were not Germans. As he observed Jews more, "the more sharply they became distinguished in my eyes from the rest of humanity."

In August 1914, World War I began, an event that Hitler regarded with joy. Within days of the announcement, the twenty-five-year-old Hitler had enlisted in the German army. Hitler took part in the battles raging across western Europe. He rose to the rank of corporal and was wounded in the legs by a shell burst. Back in Germany to recover from his wounds, he was infuriated by civilian unrest and complaints about the war. Germany's war effort, he determined, was being weakened by Jews.

In 1918, Hitler was in Germany recovering from war strain when Germany finally agreed to an armistice on November 11. "There followed terrible days and even worse nights," Hitler later wrote. "In these nights hatred grew in me, hatred for those responsible for this deed."

Those responsible, Hitler decided, were the Jews.

A Growing Hatred

When the victorious Allies dealt with the defeated Germany, they were determined to make Germany pay for the war. The notorious Versailles Treaty forced Germany to accept responsibility for the war and pay huge reparations.

The treaty caused bitterness and economic unrest across Germany. Outbreaks of violence rocked the nation as different groups tried to seize control of the government. Communists and Socialists (called Marxists by Hitler) led violent rebellions that were crushed by groups of former generals and soldiers. The army was a prominent force in putting down the Marxists, and Hitler was recruited to speak to army soldiers about the dangers of Marxism. He delivered angry, loud speeches to the soldiers, blaming the Marxists and Jews for Germany's defeat in the war. Many of the soldiers, seeking someone else to blame, agreed with Hitler.

In late 1919, Hitler went to Munich to investigate the German Workers' Party. Hitler read a pamphlet about the group, which urged a strong government and the rejection of Jews. Hitler, delighted, became a member and was put in charge of recruitment. He delivered passionate, intense speeches to crowded beer halls. Hitler rose to higher positions in the party, which at that time numbered only three thousand members.

In 1920 Hitler chose a symbol—the swastika—for the party and changed the name of the party to the National Socialist German Workers' Party (NSDAP). The members were called

Nazis. On February 24, 1920, the NSDAP formulated its platform in twenty-five points. They included the idea that the Aryan race was supreme and that the Jews were to be excluded from the German Volk community.

In November 1923, Hitler led a revolt that collapsed within hours. Hitler was tried, found guilty, and sentenced to five years in prison. He stayed only nine months, and he used the time to dictate his ideas and biography into the book, Mein Kampf (My Struggle).

Learning from the failed revolt, Hitler resolved to build a movement that would seize control of the government. However, Hitler and the Nazis had a problem. Few paid attention to him because times were good—the economy was strengthening and the sting of defeat was fading.

In 1929, however, the collapse of the stock market in New York brought the economic growth to an end. Millions lost their jobs, and the German economy appeared on the verge of collapse. Suddenly, the Nazi movement began to attract followers again. This time, however, it was not just the unemployed and the poor. Large industrialists turned to Hitler as a figure who could restore order.

With this support, the number of Germans who voted for the Nazis jumped in the 1930 election from 810,000 to 6,409,000. In July 1932, the Nazis tallied 14 million votes and became the largest party in the German parliament, which is called the Reichstag. Hitler maneuvered expertly over the next six months. On January 30, 1933, Hitler became chancellor of Germany, completing his unlikely and extraordinary rise to the most powerful position in the nation.

Many of Germany's 525,000 Jews were terrified when Hitler seized power, but only 38,000 fled the country. Germany was a rich, sophisticated country with deep traditions of art,

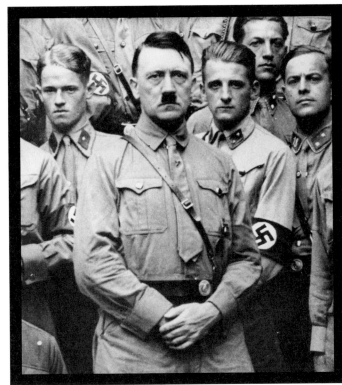

Adolf Hitler poses with a group of Nazis soon after his appointment as chancellor of Germany in 1933.

music, philosophy, and technology. Jews had been an essential part of German culture. Jews had served loyally in the German army during World War I. They had held important positions in government and industry. Yes, there might be additional discomfort and rudeness to deal with, perhaps even some unfair laws, but what could Hitler really do?

Seeds of Evil

With Germany under Nazi control, however, Hitler began to put into effect a plan to eliminate the Jews. In the medieval walled city of Nuremberg, Hitler announced legal codes designed to separate the Jews from Germans—the Nuremberg laws. Ultimately, about four hundred laws and decrees against Jews were passed. The first laws identified a "non-Aryan" as someone who had at least a Jewish grandparent. Laws forbade Jews from serving in government positions, on juries, or as commercial judges. Jewish doctors and dentists were banned from state hospitals. The Law Against the Overcrowding of German Schools and Institutions of Higher Learning allowed about one student out of one hundred to be Jewish. Others, to prove they weren't Jewish, had to produce elaborate family trees with official birth records.

The Nazis soon forbade the government from employing any non-Aryans whatsoever. The Reich Chamber of Culture was established to expel Jews from any influence in the nation's theater, film industry, or art world. The *Deutsche Allgemeine Zeitung* editorialized on April 27, 1933, that "a self-respecting nation cannot leave its higher activities in the hands of people of racially foreign origin."

While these laws were put into place, Nazis systematically isolated Jews socially. Brown-shirted Nazis in polished black boots stood outside Jewish shops and posted signs: "Germans! Protect Yourselves! Don't buy from Jews!"

Jewish schoolchildren became objects of fear and hatred. "Suddenly I had no friends," remembered Hilma Geffen-Ludomer, a young student who attended school in a Berlin suburb. "I had no more girlfriends, and many neighbors were afraid to talk to us. Some of the neighbors that we visited told me: 'Don't come anymore because I'm scared. We should not have contact with Jews.'"

In 1939 the German army attacked Poland and World War II began. Over the next year, Hitler enjoyed a number of successes that shocked the world. German armies conquered Denmark, Norway, and Holland; German tanks overwhelmed France. Convinced that victory would take only months, Hitler ordered

During the movement to boycott Jews in Germany in 1933, four Nazis sing in front of the Berlin branch of Woolworth Co. because they believe the founder was Jewish.

the invasion of the Soviet Union. In June 1941, a massive German offensive crashed into the Soviet Union, quickly occupied enormous territory, and brought many of Europe's Jews—2.5 million were still in eastern Europe at that time—under Nazi control. These developments made possible Hitler's plans to wipe out the Jewish race. Nazi leaders called this process the Final Solution.

The Killing Units: Einsatzgruppen

As German armies smashed through the Soviet Union, Hitler put into motion his plans to clear the eastern territories of all undesirable peoples—especially Jews. Once the area was cleared, German settlers would be moved in to occupy the territory and transform it into a "Garden of Eden."

The first mass killings occurred in the summer of 1941. Special groups of German soldiers—called Einsatzgruppen—began systematically removing Jews from villages and executing them. On July 11, a German officer issued detailed orders about the executions. "The shootings are to take place away from cities, villages, and thoroughfares. The graves are to be leveled in such a way that no pilgrimage site can arise. I forbid photographing and the permitting of spectators at the executions. Executions and grave sites are not to be made known."

The officer recognized that shooting women and children might be difficult for some of the men. "The battalion and company commanders are especially to provide for the spiritual care of the men who participate in this action. The impressions of the day are to be blotted out through the holding of social events in the evenings. Furthermore the men are to be instructed continuously about the political necessity of the measures."

Within a week of the German invasion of the Soviet Union, more Jews were murdered than had been killed in the entire eight-year reign of Nazism in Germany. The swiftness of the German advance, the remoteness of the territory, and the confusion of war gave the Nazi units the necessary cover to commit these acts. Thousands of Jewish men, women, children, and infants were shot at close range, often over pits filled with other victims.

These kinds of killings peaked in 1941 and 1942. The historian Christopher Browning did a detailed study of what this campaign was like for a single unit. At dawn, July 13, 1942, a column of trucks carrying German policemen pulled up outside the Polish village of Józefów. The policemen jumped out of the back of the truck and assembled around their leader, Major Wilhelm Trapp. Trapp fought back tears as he explained their assignment. Inside the sleeping village were 1,800 Jews, he explained. The Jewish men were to be separated from the women, children, and elderly. The men would be sent to a work camp. The Jewish women, children, and elderly, said Trapp, were to be shot. Trapp explained how this was necessary for the war effort, and how German civilians were being bombed in their cities by enemy airplanes. Acknowledging that this might be unpleasant, Trapp said anyone who did not want to participate could drop out.

The families were awakened and driven stumbling from their beds. They gathered in the market square and the working-age men separated from the rest. Groups of women, children, and elderly were then marched into the nearby woods. The crash of rifle volleys sounded and drifted over the town to the square where the other Jews were kept waiting. The sudden apprehension, the nauseating fear, and possibly frantic denial arose in a large cry in the marketplace. Then, however, they settled into a calm silence that startled observers.

Another historian, Daniel Goldhagen, described what actually happened as the killing units proceeded.

> Bear in mind, always, the horror of what the Germans were doing. Anyone in a killing detail who himself shot or who witnessed his comrades shoot Jews was immersed in scenes of unspeakable horror. . . . Blood, bone, and brain were flying about, often landing on the killers, smirching their faces and staining their clothes. Cries and wails of people awaiting their imminent slaughter or consumed in death throes reverberated in German ears. Such scenes—not the antiseptic descriptions that mere reportage of a killing operation presents— constituted the reality for many perpetrators.

Jews are captured in Poland in 1943 by the Nazis and marched away for deportation. The woman in the front, clearly shocked and horrified, walks with her mother-in-law, daughter, and husband. Of the four, only the man survived.

Outside the Soviet city of Kiev, on September 29 and 30, 1941, more than thirty thousand Jews were shot in a series of massacres. Even before this slaughter, a high-ranking German officer, Reinhard Heydrich, wrote to his superior, Heinrich Himmler, "It may be safely assumed that in the future there will be no more Jews in the annexed Eastern Territories."

The Final Solution

The Nazis intended far more than the destruction of Jews in eastern Europe. Hitler and his top advisers were now resolved to solve the "Jewish Question" once and for all, and all Jews in Europe were targeted. To murder such a large number of people required more than shooting squads. Instead, the Nazis decided to employ killing methods they had first used on handicapped and mentally retarded Germans and Poles in the late 1930s and early 1940s—gas.

Hitler had determined that the handicapped and mentally retarded were inferior, weakened the German race, and therefore should not be allowed to live. One method of execution was to place the victims in a sealed chamber on a truck and pump poisonous gas fumes into the chamber until the occupants were dead. Using this as a model, the Nazis began constructing several camps in Poland. These camps were designed solely for mass murder. The camps were at Treblinka, Sobibor, Majdanec, Belzec, Chelmno, and the Birkenau section of Auschwitz-Birkenau.

Before the Jews were sent to these camps, they were crowded into areas of cities that were walled off. In these ghettos—such as in Warsaw and Lodz—the occupants were given little food or medicine and many died. Over time, as the Final Solution progressed, the ghettos were cleaned out and the inhabitants forced onto transport trains that carried them to death camps or work camps.

Poland was crisscrossed with railways, with hubs to the smallest towns. The railway system could move thousands, even hundreds of thousands, of people relatively efficiently. Just as important, the Polish countryside was pocketed with thick woods far from population centers. It was an easy place to put a camp without gathering too much attention.

The railways, like a giant spiderweb stretching across Europe, carried transports of Jews. Over a period of three and a half years, according to one historian, 147 trains from Hungary,

This is a map of Nazi Germany showing the locations of
some of the major extermination and concentration camps.

87 from Holland, 76 from France, 63 from Slovakia, 27 from
Belgium, 23 from Greece, 11 from Italy, 7 from Bulgaria, and 6
from Croatia, delivered human cargoes to the Nazi camps.

Hubert Pfoch was a young German soldier traveling with
his unit to fight in Russia when his train pulled up next to
another train filled with men, women, and children. Pfoch
wrote in his diary what he saw next.

> We heard the rumor that these people were a Jewish transport. They
> call out to us that they have been traveling without food or water for
> two days. And then, when they are being loaded into the cattle cars,
> we became witnesses of the most ghastly scenes. The corpses of those
> killed the night before were thrown by Jewish auxiliary police on to a

lorry [truck] that came and went four times. The guards cram 180
people into each car—parents into one, children into another, they
didn't care how they separated families. They scream at them, shoot
and hit them so viciously that some of their rifle butts break. When
all of them are finally loaded there are cries from all cars—"Water,"
they plead, "my gold ring for water." When some of them manage to
climb out through the ventilating holes, they are shot the moment
they reach the ground—a massacre that made us sick to our souls, a
blood-bath such as I had never dreamed.

The Germans treated each transport differently, depending on
where the Jews came from. For the Jews coming from western
Europe, the guards acted almost courteously. Many of these Jews
had become a part of European society. Some thought of
themselves as French, German, or Dutch first, and then Jewish.

The object was not to allow the victims to suspect what was
about to happen. If they knew their fate, the entire transport
might have revolted as soon as the doors rolled open.
Understanding this, the Nazis took great pains to conceal their
intentions until it was too late. The Jews were told that they were
being "resettled" to a new region. Accordingly, they were
allowed to bring along suitcases filled with food and goods.

At Treblinka the commander ordered the construction of a
fake railroad station. Ticket windows, arrows, and names of
places were painted on the walls. It was meant to fool people in
the transports into believing that they had arrived at a camp
between trains. At Treblinka even a clock was put up, though the
hands never moved.

Most transports arrived at the camps full of exhausted people
who had not eaten or drunk water for days. Stanislaw Szmajzner,
his parents, his brother, older sister, and other relatives were on a
train that pulled into Sobibor, Poland, in May 1942.

When the door of our car was pushed open, all we could think of was
to get out into the air. What I saw first was two guards with whips.
They immediately began to shout, "Out!" "Out!" and hit blindly at
those who stood in front. Of course, this made everyone move quickly;
those in the back pushed towards the front, and those in front, the
immediate target of the whips, jumped off as quickly as they could. It
was all perfectly planned to get us out of the cars with no delay. They
only opened three cars at a time—that, too, was part of the system.
When I jumped down with my family, I immediately caught hold of
my brother's and little nephew's hands. I even shouted "We must stick
together." My older cousin also managed to stay with us but we
immediately lost sight of my father. We looked around desperately, but
the hurry, the noise, the fear and confusion were indescribable; it was
impossible to find anyone once we lost them from sight. About twenty

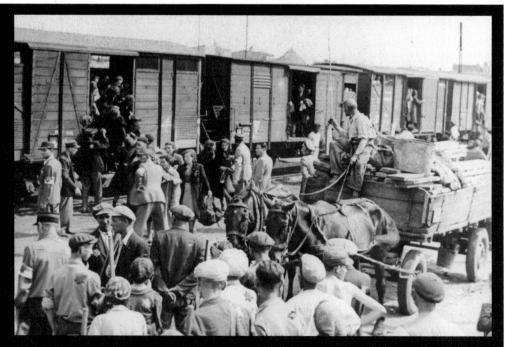

Almost all victims of the Holocaust were transported in cramped,
unsanitary train cars like these. In this image (taken between
1942 and 1944), Jews from the Lodz ghetto in Poland board
deportation trains that are heading for the Chelmno death camp.

meters away, across the square, I saw a line of SS officers and they were shooting. The purpose was to get us all to run in one direction; through a gate and a kind of corridor into yet another square.

At Treblinka the arriving people were told to hand over all their valuables. They were then separated—with men going into one barracks and women and children into another. They were then ordered to undress. Naked, the men and women were lined in rows and forced to run down a fenced-in path that was called "the tube" or "the funnel." At the end of the tube was a large chamber labeled as showers, where the people were told they were going to be disinfected.

"Some of the people from the transport had an idea what was going on, and they know already that they will not stay alive," recalled Abraham Bomba, who was pulled out of a transport to become a worker at the camp. "Pushing the people—they didn't want to or they knew already where they go—toward this big door. The crying and the hollering and the shouting that was going on over there! It was impossible. The hollering and the crying was in your ears and your mind for days and days, and at night the same thing. From the howling you couldn't even sleep a couple of nights."

Once the chamber doors were closed, carbon monoxide gas was pumped inside until everyone was dead. The bodies were then removed by a work crew of Jews (*Sonderkommando*) and buried in giant trenches.

In the Death Camps

Those who were kept alive lived in constant fear that they would be picked next or that a guard would single them out or that a mistake or small gesture could get them pulled aside and shot. One prisoner, Richard Glazar, carried a shaving kit all the time. He shaved to keep himself looking clean, sometimes seven times a day. When the prisoners were gathered for morning roll call, it was important to look clean and healthy.

"And yet, this was one of the most torturing uncertainties; one never knew how the mood of the Germans 'ran'—whether if one was seen shaving or cleaning one's boots, that wouldn't get one killed," recalled Glazar. "It was an incredible daily roulette; you see, one SS might consider a man looking after himself in this way as making himself 'conspicuous'—the cardinal sin—and then another might not. The effect of being clean always helped—it even created a kind of respect in them. But to be seen doing it might be considered showing off, or toadying, and provoke punishment, or death." Glazar, who was interviewed by a British journalist more than twenty years after the war ended, said he still carried his shaving kit.

Several Jews were kept alive at Treblinka as "work Jews"— carpenters, tailors, cooks, even musicians. In one incident, a work Jew named Blau knocked on the door to the office of Franz Stangl, the camp commander. Blau explained that his father was coming the next morning on a transport. Could Stangl do anything? The man's father was eighty years old. "Really, Blau, you must understand, it's impossible," answered Stangl. "A man of eighty . . ."

Blau asked if he could avoid having his father gassed. Instead, he would take him to a fake hospital, called the Lazarett, where prisoners were killed quickly. Blau had one more request: Could he take his father to the kitchen and give him a last meal?

"You go and do what you think best, Blau," answered Stangl. "Officially, I don't know anything, but unofficially you can tell the Kapo I said it was all right."

Blau returned the next day to Stangl's office with tears in his eyes. "I want to thank you. I gave my father a meal. And I've just taken him to the Lazarett. It's all over. Thank you very much."

"Well, Blau, there's no need to thank me," Stangl replied, "but of course if you want to thank me, you may."

Stangl recounted this conversation in 1971 to journalist Gitta Sereny, who was so disgusted that she almost halted the interview altogether. "The story represented to me the starkest example of a corrupted personality I had ever encountered," she later wrote.

Sereny was interviewing Stangl because she, like the historians Browning and Goldhagen, wanted to understand what kind of person could preside over a mass murder of hundreds of thousands. In her encounters, Stangl was polite, respectful, well mannered, and earnest, but he also seemed incapable of expressing true remorse or having an understanding of what he had done. Stangl recounted several warm anecdotes about his personal kindness to individual Jews who worked closely with him at Treblinka. But when Sereny pressed him to know whether they survived—or whether he had done anything to protect them—he kept answering, "I don't know." What happened to Blau? "I don't know."

Stangl's answer, though evasive, also contains some truth. The Germans committed genocide because of Nazi leadership, propaganda, and ancient prejudices against the Jews, as well as a cultural tendency for individual Germans to respect and obey their government. It is important to understand these reasons because it makes it easier to spot future genocides before they occur and, hopefully, prevent them.

However, on some level we can never completely understand how an individual participates in the violent act of genocide. Sereny hoped to gain some insight into this mind-set when she interviewed Stangl and published their conversations in a book, *Into That Darkness*. Did she succeed? The title comes from a poem by Edgar Allan Poe, who used the phrase to describe a confrontation with death and meaninglessness. By choosing this line for her book, Sereny is acknowledging that Stangl and the evil he committed are in some ways beyond our understanding. As Stangl said, "I don't know."

"Arbeit Macht Frei"

By 1942 the Nazis had constructed their largest concentration camp—Auschwitz. Unlike Treblinka, Auschwitz had a sizable working population (the gate to the camp carried the slogan: *Arbeit Macht Frei*—"Work Brings Freedom"). When transports arrived, many went through "selection." An SS officer would look over each prisoner and gesture to the right or to the left. Young healthy men and women—who were judged capable of doing work—were sent in one direction. The elderly, many women, and young children were sent in the other.

The fate of those sent to the left was similar to the victims at Treblinka. However, at Auschwitz, the Germans had perfected their killing technique. They constructed giant underground gas chambers with fake showerheads. The people were told to take off their clothes in a large dressing room. To keep them from understanding what was happening, they were told to remember exactly where they had placed their clothing, so they could find it after the shower.

Once in the gas chamber, the airtight doors were closed and Zyklon B gas crystals, an insecticide, were dropped through vents. After a half hour, a ventilation system pumped the gas out of the chamber. The bodies were then removed and transported to a crematorium, where they were placed in ovens and cremated (before summer 1942, however, most bodies were buried in mass graves). The ash was dumped in a nearby pond or river. Five crematories were built at Auschwitz; the largest two had thirty ovens and could burn up to five thousand bodies every day.

"Everyday we saw thousands and thousands of innocent people disappear up the chimney," recalled Filip Mueller, a Jew who worked at Auschwitz. "There they came, men, women, and children, all innocent. They suddenly vanished and the world said nothing! We felt abandoned. By the world, by humanity."

What was in the minds of those who faced the gas chambers? Rudolf Hoess, the Nazi commander at Auschwitz, wrote an account of his time at the camp before he was tried and executed. He often watched transports enter the gas chambers, and he noted that few were aware of what was about to happen. However, he recalled seeing some women with children realize that they were all about to be killed. At these moments, Hoess's description becomes almost respectful. "Even with the fear of death all over their faces, [the mothers] still managed enough strength to play with their children and talk to them lovingly."

When another transport was entering the chambers, a woman with four children, all holding hands, stepped close to Hoess and whispered: "How can you murder these beautiful, darling children? Don't you have any heart?" But another prisoner, this time an elderly man, showed rage. "Germany will pay a bitter penance for the mass murder of the Jews," he told Hoess.

Elie Wiesel arrived at Auschwitz when he was fifteen years old. He passed through selection by telling the officer he was eighteen. Wiesel and his father were with a group of men marching toward a burning pit. As they came closer, they saw

This large room was used as one of the gas chambers at the concentration camp in Auschwitz in Poland.

that the pit contained children. Wiesel turned to his father in astonishment and said it wasn't possible—people aren't simply burned to death in this age. Humanity, he said, would never tolerate it.

"Humanity? Humanity is not concerned with us," his father answered. "Today, anything is possible, even these crematories." The men began to mutter among themselves about rebelling. Wiesel considered running and throwing himself onto a nearby electric fence to die, rather than be burned alive. Others began reciting the Hebrew prayer for the dead. Just steps from the burning pit, the group was ordered to turn left and march into a barracks.

"Never shall I forget that night, the first night in camp, which has turned my life into one long night," he later wrote.

"Never shall I forget that smoke. Never shall I forget the little faces of the children, whose bodies I saw turned into wreaths of smoke beneath a silent blue sky. . . . Never shall I forget those moments which murdered my God and my soul and turned my dreams to dust. Never shall I forget these things, even if I am condemned to live as long as God Himself. Never."

Liberation

In early 1945, the German Reich was crumbling under the combined onslaughts of the Soviets from the east and the British and Americans from the west. As the Allied armies approached, the SS ordered many of the prisoners to camps deeper inside Germany. Often the weak prisoners were forced to

Piles of human bones and skulls were found at the Nazi concentration camp of Majdanek in Poland after the camp's liberation by Allied troops.

march for hours in bitter cold. Those who could not keep up were shot. Those who survived were crowded in with other prisoners at camps that could barely hold them. Without medicine or food, more died. Their bodies were left unburied. Survivors were left to starve by German troops who attempted to escape as Allied troops closed in. In this condition, camps were discovered by advancing Allied armies in spring 1945.

Journalist Edward R. Murrow recalled his experience of newly liberated Buchenwald during a broadcast on April 15, 1945. "I pray you to believe what I said about Buchenwald," he told the audience. "I have reported what I saw and heard, but only part of it. For most of it I have no words."

These men were victims and survivors of Germany's Buchenwald concentration camp, which was liberated by Allied troops in 1945. Among them is Elie Wiesel (seventh from the left on the middle bunk next to the vertical post), who went on to become an internationally famous writer.

from nuremberg to the killing fields of cambodia

although Lemkin had been warning about genocide for twenty years, even he couldn't conceive the full extent of the horrors that had occurred in Europe. When he traveled to Nuremberg, Germany, in 1946, he learned that of fifty-three family members in Poland, forty-nine were dead.

Lemkin was not just in Nuremberg to learn about his family. He hoped to influence a war tribunal that had set up its court in the ancient German city to judge and pass sentence on former Nazi officials for war crimes. Hitler had committed suicide just days before the war ended, but other top Nazis had been captured, arrested, and charged. Such a court was virtually unprecedented, and Lemkin saw it as an opportunity to get his word—*genocide*—into the vocabulary of international law.

International law is extremely complex, but for our purposes, it is important to remember one basic concept—sovereignty. The modern world is mostly organized as nations. Each nation is recognized as being sovereign; that is, it is allowed to run its affairs without direct interference from other nations. This is the bedrock of international law. A country can't simply invade another country if there is no legitimate reason to do so. But what about when a country starts murdering its own citizens? Lemkin brought this up to his professor when he was a young student. The professor used the example of a farmer killing his own chickens. The farmer had the right to do as he pleased with his own chickens on his own farm. In other words, the law that prevents one country from attacking another is stronger than any obligation to a higher law—such as human rights.

Lemkin thought that this was completely wrong. He argued that countries are most obligated to intervene in other countries when these kinds of actions are occurring. This was a radical idea. When countries attack others, they are making war. Lemkin's concept seemed to encourage the idea that war is justified to stop genocide.

Sitting in a box surrounded by guards, the Nazi defendants at the Nuremberg trials await justice. Hermann Göring (front left), one of the main leaders of Nazi Germany, worriedly leans forward and chews on his fingernails. Later, he was sentenced to death but avoided execution by committing suicide in his cell in 1946.

At Nuremberg Lemkin cornered lawyers and judges and spoke to them about his concepts. Some brushed him off, and others listened patiently, but his ideas were not accepted. When the Nazis were charged with crimes, it did not include the ones they had perpetrated on other Germans. By this logic, the Nazis could be found guilty for murdering Polish Jews, but not German Jews.

Nonetheless, Lemkin did win some victories. His relentless lobbying led to the use of the word *genocide* in one of the indictments, the first mention of the word in an international legal setting. However, when the Nuremberg tribunal finished, the Nazis were convicted of various crimes against peace and humanity, but genocide was not among them. Lemkin later called it "the blackest day" of his life, but he did not sink into despair. Hearing that the new world organization—the United Nations—was meeting in New York, he hurried aboard a flight back to the United States.

"We Must Change the World!"

In 1946 the United Nations was still in its infancy and Lemkin was determined that preventing genocide be included among the priorities of the new world body. Passionate, intense, and tireless, Lemkin pursued the individuals at the UN with what one writer called a "relentless appetite for rejection." He pigeonholed reporters and pitched endless variations on stories about genocide. When some grew weary and tried to avoid him, he chased down the halls after them, saying, "You and I, we must change the world!"

This time, Lemkin found a more willing audience. The war, the slaughter in Eastern Europe, and the images of concentration camps were still in people's minds. Lemkin, after all, had been warning this was going to happen long before World War II even started. Many delegates at the UN recognized this. In December 1946, the UN General Assembly passed a resolution that condemned genocide:

> Genocide is a denial of the right of existence of entire human groups, as homicide is the denial of the right to live of individual human beings; such denial of the right of existence shocks the conscience of mankind, results in great losses to humanity in the form of cultural and other contributions represented by these human groups, and is contrary to moral law and to the spirit and aims of the United Nations.

Lemkin was satisfied with this result, but it was by no means the end of his efforts. The key, to him, was to make genocide against the law. This came back, however, to a familiar problem—whose law? Each country had its own laws, which applied within its own borders. And one country was not supposed to meddle with another's internal laws.

Times, however, had changed. Many world leaders believed that the former way of doing things would not work in the future. Nations had to be ready to cooperate on an international level to resolve their differences. Another lesson was that one nation could not simply ignore what was happening in another country. If the various peoples of the world could agree on at least one thing, it was that another Holocaust should not be permitted.

This was the atmosphere in which the UN was founded and where Raphael Lemkin hoped to make his greatest mark. He wanted genocide to be against the law—a law that obligated one nation to intervene in another if genocide was occurring; a law that would make anyone who committed genocide a fugitive in the world community. A colleague argued to Lemkin that law meant nothing. What dictator, the colleague said, would obey a piece of paper? "Only man has law," Lemkin replied with characteristic passion. "Law must be built, do you understand me? You must build the law!"

Lemkin broadened his studies on genocide. He researched any group that had been targeted because of its race or beliefs. These cases occurred over centuries—to Aztecs and Incas massacred by Spanish explorers, to French Huguenot Protestants persecuted by French Catholic authorities, to the Armenians slaughtered in the Ottoman Empire.

Largely because of Lemkin's efforts, the UN declared on December 9, 1948, that genocide was a crime when any act was committed with "intent to destroy, in whole or in part, a national, ethical, racial, or religious group." This included murder, acts of physical brutality and mental distress, deliberate starvation or other acts to destroy life, attempts to prevent births in the group, or the forcible transferal of children of the group to another group.

In an emotional ceremony in Paris, Lemkin watched as fifty-five delegates voted to approve the law, with none voting against. After receiving congratulations from various world leaders for his efforts, Lemkin retreated to a dark hall and wept. He gently rebuffed approaching journalists, telling them to "leave me sit here alone." His efforts had left him exhausted and deathly ill, but he could claim victory. He would later write that the law meant that his mother "and many millions did not die in vain."

But just what had Lemkin achieved? If genocide was occurring in a country, other countries were obligated to take measures to stop it. If this failed, however, nations could use force and intervene in another country's internal borders. This was virtually unprecedented, and it created a new emphasis on law among nations, not just within them. "Relating to the sacred right of existence of human groups we are proclaiming today the supremacy of international law once and forever," said one official.

The Struggle for Ratification

With the passage of the law, however, it still had to be submitted and ratified, or formally approved, by each country's government. Many governments did ratify the law, but one in particular did not—the United States.

In the 1950s, the United States occupied an unfamiliar position as a world superpower. Many Americans, however, urged that the country return to a period of isolationism (as in the 1920s and 1930s) and not worry about the world's problems. Others urged confrontation with the other world power—the Soviet Union—and its system of Communism. These tensions erupted in criticisms of the genocide convention.

Some thought the law was too vague. After all, how many people had to be killed from a group before it could be declared genocide? Others wondered whether U.S. government treatment of Native Americans in the 1800s could also be punished under the law. Southern lawmakers grew concerned that segregation—laws that separated blacks and whites in social settings in many southern states—and lynchings of African Americans might also be considered genocide. Others refused to give up American sovereignty, or the right to dictate what happens within U.S. borders, to an international organization.

Lemkin went to work again. He knew that without U.S. participation, the law was doomed. The United States had not joined the League of Nations in the 1920s and 1930s, and as a result, the organization had largely failed. He sent letters to senators; he confronted lawmakers in the halls of the Capitol in Washington, D.C. As he had before the war, he spoke to small groups of concerned citizens—virtually anyone who would listen.

But the optimism and hope for international law that had bloomed following World War II faded. Lemkin's countless letters and personal appeals drew little or no response. An effort to write a four-volume work on genocide failed to win attention from publishers. Lemkin grew more frustrated and exhausted. On August 28, 1959, in New York City, he died of a sudden heart attack. Lemkin and the genocide law dropped from the U.S. political scene.

In January 1967, more than seven years after Lemkin's death, Wisconsin senator William Proxmire stood up in a nearly empty Senate chamber and gave a speech. He declared that the Senate's failure to ratify the genocide convention was a "national shame," and he was determined to give a speech each day urging the ratification.

Proxmire was a senator who had known defeat—he had run for the Wisconsin governorship three times and lost. But he was also cheerful even after repeated failures, and he never quit. The genocide convention was brought to his attention in the mid-1960s by a human rights lawyer. When Proxmire learned that seventy nations had ratified the genocide law and that the U.S. Senate had not, he was shocked. To Proxmire, it was inexcusable, and thus he resolved to start giving speeches in the Senate on a daily basis. In 1967 alone, he gave 199 different speeches on the genocide convention.

Proxmire persisted through the late 1960s and into the mid-1970s, when disturbing news emerged that a genocide was

U.S. senator William Proxmire campaigned repeatedly in the 1960s and 1970s to urge the United States to ratify the genocide law.

occurring in Southeast Asia. In the early 1960s, the United States had intervened in a decadeslong civil war between North and South Vietnam. American policy makers supported South Vietnam against the Communist North, and when it appeared that South Vietnam was going to fall to the Communists, more than 500,000 U.S. soldiers were dispatched to fight. The result was a bloody quagmire that left the United States bitterly divided and North Vietnam undefeated. After suffering more than 50,000 dead, the United States withdrew its forces. South Vietnam collapsed just a few years later.

Even after the collapse of South Vietnam, peace did not come to the region. In one of South Vietnam's neighboring countries, Cambodia, a civil war still raged. Communist groups called the Khmer Rouge fought the government. In 1975 the Cambodian government was defeated and the Khmer Rouge seized power. Clad in black clothing, red and white-checkered

Khmer Rouge fighters celebrate the government takeover on April 17, 1975, as they enter Phnom Penh, the capital city of Cambodia.

scarves, and sandals made from old tires, Khmer Rouge soldiers entered the country's capital city, Phnom Penh.

A Young Girl in Cambodia

Loung Ung was just five years old at the time. She was bewildered by mud-streaked trucks carrying the young soldiers, who pumped their fists skyward in elation. She walked home and asked her father, who was a captain in the military police, who the men were and why they were here. "They want us," he answered.

The Khmer Rouge were Communists who believed that people could be tainted—or corrupted—by exposure to different ideas, especially from the capitalist West. In very simple terms, the Communists were trying to create a society in which no one competed against another and all people worked for the common good. In theory, this meant that there were no rich to exploit the poor, and people would not starve or be left without the means to support themselves. Capitalism, said Communists, was designed to crush the workers for the enrichment of a tiny minority.

But Communism had proved extremely difficult to create in reality. Some people refused to give up their property or to obey

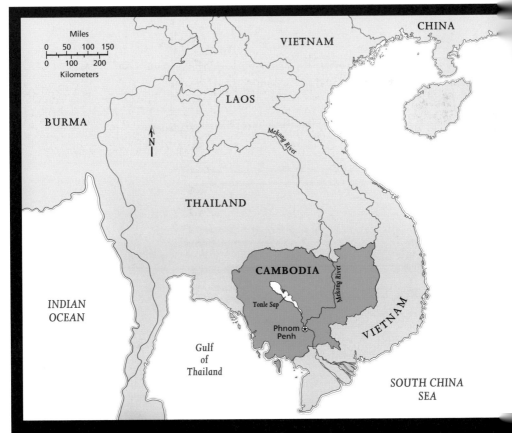

This map shows the location of Cambodia and its capital city, Phnom Penh.

the Communists. Some people worked too hard; others, too little. The Communist government was supposed to organize the economy, but leaders often made bad decisions and couldn't manage a complex system in which millions of people exchanged goods every day.

One of the problems, said Communists, was that some people actively worked against the Communist system. These people had been exposed to capitalist ideas and thus wouldn't give up their greedy desires to get rich or to undermine the Communist government. This thinking, according to the Khmer Rouge, meant that illiterate peasants in the countryside were more pure than the occupants of a city—the "bourgeois"— where people had been exposed to the ideas of the capitalist elements.

The solution, the Khmer Rouge ultimately decided, was to rid the society of these corrupt elements—to purify the system by eliminating the people who were holding it back. This meant either "reeducating" people about their faults or getting rid of the people altogether. "They were killing anyone who wore glasses, because if they wore glasses it suggested they knew how to read, and if they knew how to read, it suggested they had been infected with the bourgeois virus," recalled Congressman Stephen Solarz, who traveled to Southeast Asia after the Khmer Rouge took control of Cambodia.

On April 17, 1975, on the same day that Ung saw the Khmer Rouge soldiers enter Phnom Penh, trucks carrying loudspeakers roamed through the streets, warning everyone to leave. The messages claimed that U.S. bombers were en route to destroy the city and that everyone had to evacuate. Ung, along with her parents and six siblings, joined the hundreds of thousands crowded on the highways leading into the countryside.

At checkpoints, Khmer Rouge soldiers asked questions to weed out those who had been "infected" by capitalism or who had a connection with the former rulers. Ung's father, though a military police officer, was able to convince a guard that he was in fact a farmer. They passed through, and eventually settled in a village.

A Khmer Rouge soldier waves his pistol and orders store owners to abandon their shops in Phnom Penh.

Soon after their arrival, they and several other resettled families gathered to hear a speech from the village chief, who stood with two armed guards behind him. In the village, he explained, everyone lives by strict rules. "One of our rules applies to how we dress," he continued. "As you see, we wear the same clothes. Everyone wears his or her hair in the same style. By wearing the same thing, we rid ourselves of the corrupt Western creation of vanity."

A guard snatched a bag from a woman and grimaced with disgust at the colorful clothes inside. The guards moved among the families, taking bags of modern clothing. They made a pile and set it aflame. Ung, whose prized red dress was among the pile, stared with rage and mourning.

The chief told them that their thoughts had to be cleansed. They were to drop all formal words such as *sir* or Mr. or Mrs. The chief dismissed such words as "bad habits and fancy titles" brought to Cambodia by evil foreigners. Instead, everyone was to use the word *met* preceding a person's name. Other words—such as *dad* and *mom*—were declared illegal.

"I hold on to Pa's finger even tighter as the chief rants off other new words," recalled Ung. "The new Khmer have better words for eating, sleeping, working, stranger; all designed to make us equal."

No one is allowed to own anything, said the chief. Everything is owned by the high government—Angkar. Everyone is ordered to eat together; if anyone does not work or is lazy or late for work, then he or she will receive nothing. The families were ordered to live together in houses. Children will be educated, but only in schools approved by the Angkar. "Children in our society will not attend school just to have their brains cluttered with useless information," he said. A similar message was being delivered to millions of shocked, disoriented, and terrified people across Cambodia.

Over the next months, the transplanted Cambodians—the "new people" as they were called—were put to work. They spent their days working in the rice fields and their nights listening to lectures about life under Angkar. For many of the villagers, there was no radio, no television, no newspapers, or other contact with the outside world. In many areas, food grew scarce, and the new people grew thin, dirty, and diseased. All the while, the Khmer Rouge patrolled the villages day and night. They listened for anyone whispering against the regime and sought out former soldiers or employees of the previous government. Some were able to hide their identity for months and even years, but the Khmer Rouge were relentless and ruthless. Fear and starvation spread over the countryside, and thousands of people began to disappear.

The leader of the Angkar was a shadowy and secretive figure, Saloth Sar, now known to the world as Pol Pot. Pol Pot was determined to remake Cambodia according to his twisted vision. While much of this had to do with Communism, he also believed deeply that Cambodia was to recover the power and glory it had enjoyed hundreds of years before. This meant

Cambodian Communist leader Pol Pot was responsible for the deaths of at least one million Cambodians in the 1970s.

eliminating outside influences and anyone who was not pure Cambodian.

Considering the Buddhism religion as incompatible with his program, he ordered Buddhist monks throughout the country murdered and their monasteries destroyed. A Khmer Rouge official would later explain that the Cambodian people had simply stopped believing in Buddhism and that the monks then abandoned the temples and monasteries. "The problem gradually becomes extinguished," she said. "Hence, there is no problem." Other groups in Cambodia were also systematically identified and targeted for destruction—including Chinese, Vietnamese, and Muslims. From 1975 to 1979, anyone who was not a pure Cambodian lived a precarious existence.

Ung and her family continued to work in their village, where she struggled through the days with the gnawing pain of hunger. One night, while most of the family was asleep, Ung heard her mother and father talking very quietly. The Khmer Rouge, her father told her mother, had learned of his position in the former government. So many neighbors had already vanished, and he knew that he would be next. Ung's father suggested they try to send the children to separate orphanages, where they wouldn't inform on one another and might be safe from the soldiers. Ung's mother pleaded that they were still too young, and Ung's father partially agreed. "Not now, but soon," he said.

During the next evening, Ung was admiring a lovely sunset when she saw two men dressed in black and carrying rifles approach their hut. They asked for her father. When he came out of the hut, they told him that their ox wagon was stuck in the mud a mile or two away. They needed him to help pull the wagon out.

Ung's father asked if he could have a moment with his

family. One of the soldiers nodded. He entered the hut with Ung's mother, and in a moment, Ung heard her mother quietly weeping. He reappeared through the hut door.

"Opposite the soldiers, Pa straightens his shoulders, and for the first time since the Khmer Rouge takeover, he stands tall," Ung later wrote.

> Thrusting out his chin and holding his head high, he tells the soldiers he is ready to go. Looking up he clenches his teeth. I reach up my hand and lightly tug at his pant leg. I want him to feel better about leaving us. Pa puts his hand on my head and tousles my hair. Suddenly he surprises me and picks me up off the ground. His arms tight around me, Pa holds me and kisses my hair.

> "My beautiful girl," he said. "I have to go away with these two men for a while."

Ung's father said good-bye to the rest of his children and then walked away with the two soldiers.

Ung never saw her father again, and by the time the Khmer Rouge were driven from power by an invasion from neighboring Vietnam in early 1979, her mother and youngest sister had been killed. This personal tragedy took place against the backdrop of a much larger crime: an estimated two million people had been either murdered or starved to death. Thousands of bodies were found in mass graves, the individuals either shot or bludgeoned. The invading Vietnamese soldiers uncovered a prison in Phnom Penh where sixteen thousand Cambodians had been tortured and killed for allegedly plotting against Pol Pot's regime. This prison, Tuol Sleng, also contained photographs of the prisoners before they were executed. They are the last, searing images of individuals who, within minutes or hours, would be dead.

This site near Phnom Penh held mass graves of the victims of the genocide in Cambodia. The graves were exhumed in 1980 so the remains could be used as memorials.

The victims' skulls and bones are piled up at the memorial in Choeung Ek to remember the people killed by the Khmer Rouge.

News of the events in Cambodia had been circulating through the international community for years. The United States, however, was still recovering from its painful reverse in Vietnam. Sending soldiers back into the region, which some argued for, could not gain broad support. For most Americans, the whole region was best forgotten or ignored.

However, when the Vietnamese invaded Cambodia, the United States sided with the Khmer Rouge, arguing that no country should invade another. The United States also hoped to keep favor with China, which supported the Khmer Rouge regime. In addition, the United States still considered Vietnam an enemy. Thus, despite evidence of genocide, the United States and China supported the Khmer Rouge as it fought against the new government. The Khmer Rouge continued to sit in the United Nations as the representative of Cambodia. The Khmer Rouge leaders, unlike many of the top Nazi officials in Germany, faced virtually no prosecution for their crimes.

The Convention Is Ratified

Proxmire continued to rise each day in the Senate to speak about the genocide convention. By 1980 he had given more than two thousand separate speeches, and no end seemed in sight. The arguments against the convention rarely changed. Conservatives did not believe it was in the United States' best interest to be entangled in treaties of any kind, and they pointed out that the nation's track record on human rights and the law left nothing to be ashamed of.

However, this stance exposed the United States to critics. When the United States criticized the Soviet Union for human rights abuses, the Soviet Union smugly referred back to the genocide treaty. How can you criticize us, they asked, when you have failed to sign one of the most basic treaties on human rights? These kinds of exchanges became more important after Ronald Reagan entered the White House in 1981. President Reagan was a fierce opponent of Communism, and he was not afraid to say so. He used strongly moral language, identifying the Soviet Union as an "evil empire."

In 1985, however, Reagan made a serious blunder. As part of a trip to West Germany to commemorate the fortieth anniversary of the end of World War II, Reagan was to visit a cemetery in Bitburg. Among the many buried there were forty-nine Nazi Waffen SS officials. When this was discovered, it caused an uproar. How could a U.S. president, the leader of the free world, honor men who served in the SS? Reagan's aides tried to defend him, saying that the visit would help heal the wounds of the

But Was It Genocide?

What happened in Cambodia, some say, was not genocide because the perpetrators and the victims were both of the same group. Moreover, they argue, those who died were not specifically targeted for destruction for who they were. These were Cambodians killing Cambodians. This argument, however, didn't hold up. The Khmer Rouge did, in fact, commit genocide by murdering many groups simply for who they were—e.g., ethnic Chinese, Buddhist monks, and Vietnamese. The Cambodians who were killed, it was determined by the UN, died because of their political beliefs, and this fell under the definition of genocide.

war. In any case, they said, Reagan was to meet with the West German leader, Helmut Kohl, and changing the trip would cause enormous political embarrassment for both leaders.

When he heard this, Holocaust survivor Elie Wiesel was scathing. "The issue here is not politics, but good and evil. And we must never confuse them," he told Reagan. For Reagan, who had used similar language to describe the Soviet Union, the rebuke was stinging. However, Reagan would not back down. Ultimately, he visited the cemetery and a concentration camp, despite protests.

Then there was another development. Suddenly the White House grew very interested in the genocide convention. Though previous presidents had spoken in favor of the genocide treaty in principal, it was Reagan who provided the necessary support to get it passed. Conservatives were aware that Reagan's support meant the treaty would be accepted, but they were determined to water down provisions that made U.S. citizens susceptible to the International Court of Justice. This organization had been formed to prosecute perpetrators of war crimes and genocide. To the conservatives, however, it meant a world court that could prosecute Americans, and they considered this a serious threat to U.S. sovereignty.

In February 1986, the United States became the ninety-eighth nation to ratify the treaty. The opposing senators, however, had succeeded in making the treaty much weaker than originally planned. This debate about the role of a world court would deepen over the next decade.

chapter five
the tutsis of rwanda

On April 6, 1994, a small private jet flew above Rwanda, in central Africa. The aircraft was about to land at Rwanda's Kigali International Airport when two missiles streaked into the sky and struck the airplane. The craft shuddered and dove into the presidential palace below. There was a flash, a clap of explosion, and silence.

The airplane had been carrying two African leaders. One was the president of Rwanda, Juvénal Habyarimana; the other was the president of the neighboring nation, Burundi, Cyprien Ntaryamira. The deaths of these two presidents led to some of the most horrific mass killings in history. Today, the Rwandans refer to the time before the airplane crash simply as "Before."

Rwanda is occupied primarily by two groups: the Hutu and the Tutsi. Most of the population—about 80 percent—is Hutu. The number of Tutsi is about 15 percent. (The remaining 5 percent is made up of other ethnicities.) Despite being a far smaller group, the Tutsi had dominated for centuries. They owned cattle, a symbol of wealth and power. The Hutu labored in farm fields, hoping one day to scrape together enough money to buy cows of their own and rise to the wealthy class.

Tension ran high between the Tutsi and Hutu. Any Hutu rebellions were crushed violently by the Tutsi. Some Hutu did accumulate the wealth necessary to join the ruling Tutsi. For most, however, it was an unrealizable dream.

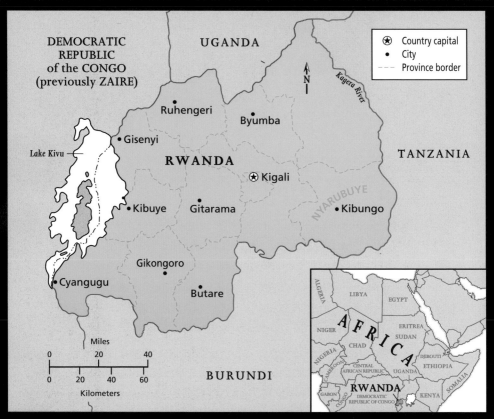

This map shows the location of Rwanda in Africa, as well as major cities and borders of the provinces during the time of the genocide in 1994.

When Europeans took over Africa in the 1800s, they exploited the division between the Tutsi and Hutu to secure their own authority. The Germans and later the Belgians favored the Tutsi. They appointed a Tutsi king and a Tutsi nobility to rule the country. For the most part, the Tutsi cooperated with the Belgians. After all, it was a relationship that enabled them to have wealth and power.

The Belgians, however, used more measures to divide Tutsi and Hutu, thus making it easier for the Belgians to rule the country. In schools children were taught that the Tutsi were racially superior to the Hutu and that it was thus natural that they ruled the country. Tutsi individuals were favored with better jobs and positions of authority. In 1933 the Belgians issued identity cards to everyone in the country. Each card bore a stamp for Hutu or Tutsi. Among the Rwandans, these cards hardened the lines between Hutu and Tutsi. Even if Hutu amassed enough riches, they could never join the ruling class—they were marked for life.

The bitterness of this arrangement exploded in violence in 1959. When the Tutsi king died, the Hutu openly revolted. For the first time, the Belgians did little to support the Tutsi. Europeans were being forced to leave Africa, and the Belgians knew that the Hutu, who vastly outnumbered the Tutsi, would soon take power in Rwanda. By withdrawing their support from the ruling Tutsi, the Belgians were hoping to establish good relations with the Hutu.

The Tutsi found themselves besieged and attacked by crowds of Hutu. No one is certain how many Tutsi died in the violence, but estimates range from 10,000 to 100,000. Tutsi refugees fled to neighboring countries. There, they plotted their eventual return. One Tutsi group, called the Rwandan Patriotic Front (RPF), organized in Uganda.

The Hutu had taken control of Rwanda, but they feared that armed Tutsi groups (called "cockroaches" by the government) would invade in an attempt to regain power. In the minds of the Hutu, the Tutsi became objects of fear and loathing. They were denied jobs by the new government and the equal protection of the country's laws.

Through the 1960s, 1970s, and 1980s, the Tutsi in Rwanda lived uneasily with their Hutu compatriots. Whenever the economy appeared to be failing, the rulers blamed the Tutsi. In 1987 coffee prices collapsed, putting enormous pressure on the many Rwandans who grew coffee beans to make a living. Tutsi groups, especially the RPF, continued to fight against the Hutu government along the Rwandan border. The clashes sent Hutu refugees into other parts of the country, where they needed to be fed and sheltered. With the economy failing and rampant corruption in the government, this could not be done easily. The country's leaders, fearful that they were losing their grip on power, spoke louder and louder against the Tutsi, saying they were to blame for everything that was wrong in Rwandan society.

"To peasants with a long folk memory of past Tutsi misrule, the warnings and the increasingly hysterical propaganda had a powerful effect," wrote Fergal Keane, a journalist in Rwanda. "Tens of thousands became infected—and I can think of no other word that can describe the condition—by an anti-Tutsi psychosis; they were convinced through newspapers, radio and the frequent public speeches that the Tutsis were going to turn them into beasts of the field once again." The Rwandan president, Juvénal Habyarimana, created a civilian militia, along with his police force and army units, to defend the Hutu against what he called the Tutsi threat. He named this group Interahamwe, or "those who stand together."

But in 1993, Habyarimana faced an impossible situation. The economy had all but collapsed, he faced growing opposition in the government, and RPF forces were closing in on the capital. Only an intervention of French soldiers saved Habyarimana from total defeat. In August 1993, Habyarimana signed the Arusha Peace Accords, which would allow the RPF participation in the government. It seemed that a new era was dawning in Rwanda, but many of Habyarimana's closest supporters were not about to give up their privileges and share power with the hated Tutsi. It was during the return flight from one of the negotiations that Habyarimana's jet was shot down.

The Genocide Begins

News of the airplane crash spread quickly. A UN commander, Lieutenant General Romeo Dallaire, was watching television in his residence in Kigali when a telephone call alerted him to the situation. Dallaire was in Rwanda to help oversee the accords between the Rwandan government and the RPF, and he knew that Habyarimana's death threatened everything the UN was trying to achieve.

Dallaire rushed to a local military barracks, where a group of Hutu generals had already claimed power over the country. Dallaire reminded the generals that the Rwandan government existed, even if Habyarimana was dead. The lawful leader of the government, he said, was the prime minister—a statement that made the generals laugh coldly.

In the next twenty-four hours, the Hutu methodically hunted down moderate politicians (many of them Hutu) who favored the peace accords with the RPF. A leading figure, Prime Minister Uwilingiyimana, was surrounded with her husband and children by Hutu militia and shot down in a UN compound. Ten Belgian soldiers, part of Uwilingiyimana's escort, were taken prisoner and then hacked to death with machetes. The message to the international community was clear and simple: stay out.

Samuel Ndagijimana was an orderly who worked in a handsome brick hospital that sat on a hill called Mugonero. The hospital was connected to a church complex, and as tension thickened in the countryside, many Tutsi sought refuge there. Samuel saw villages burning in the distance, and each night he saw groups of Hutu gathering. "You didn't know exactly what was happening, just that there was something coming."

More than two thousand refugees crowded onto Mugonero,

with Hutu soldiers forming a tight ring around them. Many of the refugees had already escaped terrible massacres, and they had few illusions about their fate. Tutsi ministers sent notes to the Hutu leaders of the church, asking for mercy. "We wish to inform you that we have heard that tomorrow we will be killed with our families," read one. "We therefore request you to intervene on our behalf and talk with the mayor." The person who received this note would later claim that he could do nothing.

"You must be eliminated," was the response from Hutu leaders. "You must die." Another message announced that the killing would begin the next day at "exactly nine o'clock."

The leaders kept their word, and at nine the next morning, soldiers piled out of trucks and began firing guns and lobbing grenades into the crowd of Tutsi. They chanted "eliminate the Tutsis." Some of the Tutsi had gathered rocks, bricks, and sticks to try to fend off the attackers, but these were "useless,"

Refugees fleeing from Rwanda walk past groups of dead bodies lying by the side of the road.

remembered a survivor. Several Tutsi hiding in the brush could track the progress of the massacres because large flocks of birds appeared over the fresh killing sites.

An Organized Slaughter

It soon became clear that this was not a spontaneous outbreak of violence caused by a sudden plane crash. The Hutu leaders had prepared. Relying on identification cards that labeled each citizen as Hutu or Tutsi, they had methodically prepared lists of Tutsi to be eliminated. The Kagera River was used as a place to dump corpses. Thousands were killed on the banks and then pushed into the swift currents. Among the most horrific photographs of the Rwandan genocide are those of bloated corpses washed into shallows or caught in weeds or rocks.

Some Tutsi were overtaken before they realized what was happening. Others fled into the thick brush and jungle, where most were tracked down, flushed from their hiding places, and murdered. Many sought refuge in Rwanda's churches. Journalist Fergal Keane and a news crew visited the villiage of Nyarubuye, where a church and school in the Rwandan countryside was a gathering place for hundreds of Tutsi weeks before.

Keane later described seeing a white marble statue of Christ and a banner celebrating Easter outside the church. "Below that there is the body of a man lying across the steps, his knees buckled underneath his body and his arms cast behind his head." As Keane walked the grounds, he had to avoid bodies strewn along and on the path. He described dead men, women, and children who were killed by machetes or grenades.

"How many are there? I think perhaps a hundred, but it is hard to tell. The bodies seem to be melting away. Such terrible faces. Horror, fear, pain, abandonment. Here the dead have no dignity." There were many killed outside the door to the church administration office. Perhaps they believed an official could save them. Other Tutsi had fled into the church itself.

"There are bodies between the pews and another pile of bones at the foot of the statue of the Virgin Mary. In a cloister, next to the holy water fountain, a man lies with his arms over his head. He must have died shielding himself from the machete blows." The dead were left unburied at Nyarubuye as a memorial. A year after the killings and Keane's visit to the site, journalists kept returning to view the bodies, which had become skeletons.

In 1994 hundreds of Tutsi were massacred in the village of Nyarubuye, where the bodies were left outside the church as a memorial to the victims.

How could the killers commit such acts? One witness later described how groups subtly pressured and then forced individuals to join them. "Everyone was called to hunt the enemy," the witness said. "But let's say someone is reluctant. Say that guy comes with a stick. They tell him, 'No, get a masu' (a stick studded with nails). So, OK, he does, and he runs along with the rest, but he doesn't kill. They say, 'Hey, he might denounce us later. He must kill. Everyone must help to kill at least one person.' So this person who is not a killer is made to do it. And the next day it's become a game for him. You don't need to keep pushing him."

Hotel Rwanda

One man, Paul Rusesabagina, watched the violence with growing alarm. Rusesabagina, manager of the Belgian-owned Hotel des Diplomates in Kigali, was a Hutu, but his wife was Tutsi. Just days after the carnage began, he was in his home with his wife, four children, and thirty friends who had taken refuge with them. Then Rusesabagina received a message. A new government had formed and wanted to make the Hotel des Diplomates its headquarters, but the hotel and all its rooms had been locked up. Would Paul come into Kigali and open the hotel?

Rusesabagina gathered his family and friends and was driven into the city in cars filled with soldiers. Suddenly, they pulled over and a soldier turned to Rusesabagina. "Do you know that all of the owners of the other businesses have been killed? We've killed them," he said. "But you're lucky. We're not killing you today because they sent us to look for you and get you for the government." Rusesabagina sweated with nervousness as he told the men that they would gain nothing by killing him, rather he had money and they could have it. The soldier listened to Rusesabagina for an hour and agreed to take five hundred dollars. The drive into the city resumed, and Rusesabagina, his family, and friends arrived at the hotel safely.

Three days later, however, the government decided to move and Rusesabagina needed to find a new safe place. One option was another hotel, Mille Collines, where he had been a manager for several years. When the government left the Hotel des Diplomates, Rusesabagina loaded his family and friends into a van and tagged along at the back of the convoy. Since the city was still dangerous, he broke off only at the end to steer the van into the hotel Mille Collines.

The Mille Collines was the richest hotel in Kigali. When Rusesabagina arrived, it was filled with hundreds of people who had so far evaded the murderous rampages. However, it was not a question of whether they would die but when.

Rusesabagina found himself in a delicate situation. Tutsi were being murdered all over the city, and the leaders in charge of that murder often used the hotel as a meeting place or a spot to get drinks. Rusesabagina used this to his advantage. With liquor, money, and his extensive business contacts, he managed to bribe or distract many of these leaders. His priority was to protect the people in the hotel.

However, he could also be firm. "I kept telling them, 'I don't agree with what you're doing,' just as openly as I'm doing now," he told journalist Philip Gourevitch. "I'm a man who's used to saying no when I have to. That's all I did—what I felt like doing. Because I never agree with killers. I didn't agree with them. I refused, and I told them so."

One morning, Rusesabagina was woken by a lieutenant with a blunt request. Everyone in the hotel had to be evacuated within thirty minutes. Rusesabagina immediately recognized this for what it was—a death order. Desperate, he tried to stall for time. He reminded the lieutenant that the people in the hotel were refugees, and he asked him what security precautions were being taken.

"Didn't you hear what I said?" snapped the lieutenant. "We want everybody out, and within half an hour."

"I'm still in bed," he told the lieutenant, "and need a half hour to shower. I'll then get everybody out." Frantically, Rusesabagina and some trusted friends made calls to their contacts, looking for someone who might overrule the lieutenant. The thirty minutes had ticked away when an army jeep suddenly pulled up to the lieutenant. His troops were ordered to pull back. Rusesabagina peered out a hotel window and saw hundreds of soldiers and civilians, who had surrounded the hotel, leave. They were carrying guns and machetes.

Despite this close call, Rusesabagina continued to reach out to people who were still being hunted. He discovered a woman and her children cowering in their house after the radio announced that they had been killed. Relying on his contacts, Rusesabagina sent an army officer to pick her up and bring her to the hotel. The woman and her family survived.

In another situation, a man at the hotel gave an interview that was broadcast on the radio. The government heard the interview and ordered a soldier to go to the hotel, find the man, and kill him. Rusesabagina, however, refused to allow the soldiers to carry out the order.

A journalist later asked Rusesabagina a simple question— why? Why, when hundreds of thousands were committing acts of violence and terror around him, did Rusesabagina act to protect life? Remember the journalist who asked German commander Franz Stangl how he had overseen the murder of hundreds of thousands? Stangl answered, "I don't know."

Relying on his cunning bravery and connections, Paul Rusesabagina protected the lives of more than one thousand Rwandans during the genocide of the Tutsi people.

But Rusesabagina gave the same answer when asked why he saved lives. "I don't know," he told the journalist. "I don't know, but I refused so many things."

Stangl's answer suggests that people are capable of evil that is beyond our ability to comprehend. Rusesabagina's answer, however, hints at the opposite: that even in the midst of something as horrible as genocide, people are capable of heroism and good that is beyond understanding.

Rusesabagina had a phone line that the government had not yet disconnected. It was his connection to the outside world, and he sent faxes and gave interviews about the situation in Rwanda. "We sent many faxes to Bill Clinton himself at the White House," he remembered. What was the rest of the world doing as Rwanda was devastated?

International Reaction

Dallaire, the commander of a contingent of UN soldiers in Rwanda, was shocked by the first few days of murder, but he also considered them to be an uncoordinated outburst of violence—perhaps the Hutu settling old scores with political enemies. The chaos, he figured, would taper off. But on April 9, Dallaire received an urgent call from UN personnel at a church. When Dallaire's assistant reached the church, he discovered hundreds of men, women, and children had been murdered. The priests, who were Polish, said the killing had been highly organized. This was not a random act of passion or an act of war. It had been planned and executed with cold precision, and it seemed to be against all Tutsi, not just politicians or soldiers.

Dallaire sent a request to UN headquarters in New York City, asking that his force be doubled to five thousand and that he be allowed to use force to stop the killings. "Give me the means and I can do more," he wrote. Unless this support and authorization arrived, Dallaire and his small unit would be helpless.

However, the United States and other countries were not so much worried about Rwandans as they were about their citizens in the country. The United States evacuated its embassy by April 10. Bob Dole, a prominent U.S. senator, said, "The Americans are out, and as far as I'm concerned, in Rwanda, that ought to be the end of it." Dallaire received orders to remain neutral, help the evacuations, and only use force if fired upon first.

The RPF, however, was already calling the actions genocide and urged world leaders to help. "When the institution of the UN was created after the Second World War, one of its fundamental objectives was to see to it that what happened to the Jews in Nazi Germany would never happen again," wrote an

RPF representative to the head of the UN Security Council. Dallaire, watching with growing desperation as the violence rose around him, scanned a book on international law and determined that he was witnessing genocide.

The importance of the word *genocide* cannot be underestimated. If U.S. officials, after all, said genocide was in fact happening, then they would be obligated to do something about it. Over the next two months, U.S. officials refused to use the word until it became untenable. Then they settled on the phrase "acts of genocide," which legally is not the same as genocide itself.

James Woods, deputy assistant secretary for African Affairs at the Department of Defense from 1986 to 1994, testified in Congress on behalf of the Clinton administration during the genocide. The White House, however, ordered him not to use the word when answering questions from members of Congress. He later called the day "miserable."

"[It was] miserable because I think it was sort of a formal spectacle of the United States in disarray and retreat, leading the international community away from doing the right thing and I think everybody was perfectly happy to follow our lead—in retreat," Woods later said.

The United States actively pushed for the UN to withdraw the forces it had in Rwanda, which it did slowly but surely. Among the U.S. public, there were expressions of concern in the media and in Congress, but there was also a sense that there was nothing that could effectively be done. President Clinton did not hold a top-level meeting once during the entire crisis.

One reason U.S. policy makers were so reluctant was because of what had happened in Somalia at the end of 1993. U.S. soldiers had been sent to the African nation as part of a peacekeeping force. But then eighteen U.S. soldiers were killed in a fierce gun battle, and the bodies of some of them were dragged through the streets of the city of Mogadishu and mutilated. Americans were shocked by what they saw on the nightly news, and their support for the peacekeeping mission abruptly collapsed. Rwanda, in some ways, seemed to be just another example of violence flaring up on the African continent. It didn't seem worth American lives to stop the slaughter.

"The Clinton administration's policy was, 'Let's withdraw altogether. Let's get out of Rwanda. Leave it to its fate,'" writer Philip Gourevitch later said. "The political calculus from the White House's point of view was if they did the completely wrong thing in Rwanda, was there ever going to be a bill to pay for it politically? Probably not."

The Failure of Leadership

Others, however, argued that Rwanda was not just a political calculation. Many leaders in the Pentagon refused to send troops into harm's way unless there was a clear national interest at stake and only if the public and the nation's leaders fully backed the use of force. Woods said that some U.S. generals wondered, "Why is it our responsibility to send our own troops to get killed in every remote corner of the earth?"

Part of the tragedy of the Rwandan genocide was that the United States, in the mid-1990s, was undisputedly the world's only superpower. There was no longer a threat from the Soviet Union, and if the United States wanted something to be done, it could probably have done so. Rwanda, then, was a tremendous opportunity for the United States to show that it would use its power to prevent genocide.

But Rwanda caused a "considerable disillusionment" for those who hoped that U.S. power would be used to stop genocide, said Woods. "In the absence of effective leadership to explain it to [the public], why would the public rally behind sending the 82nd Airborne to a place they've never heard of to sort out ethnic quarrels between people they've never met? I think it can be explained. I think that's what leadership is all about."

Samantha Power, author of "*A Problem from Hell*": *America and the Age of Genocide,* listed many things the United States could have done, short of sending in ground troops, to delay or even stop the Rwandan genocide. It could have prevented Belgian peacekeepers from leaving the country so early. It could have urged other nations to send troops to Rwanda. U.S. officials could have denounced the slaughter and pledged that the people responsible would be held accountable. U.S. technology could have been deployed to halt the hate radio broadcasts that were largely responsible for creating an environment in which genocide could take place. "In short," wrote Power, "the United States could have led the world."

No Justice

By July 1994, an estimated eight hundred thousand Rwandan Tutsi had been slaughtered. In response to the genocide, the RPF invaded the country and drove the Hutu from power. An unprecedented period of intense violence—which at its peak exceeded the death rate of the Holocaust—calmed into simmering tension. Ever since, international leaders have tried to explain what went wrong in Rwanda and why they did not do more to help the situation.

Four years later, President Clinton visited Rwanda and apologized for his lack of action. "We in the United States and the world community did not do as much as we could have and should have done to try to limit what occurred," he said. "It may seem strange to you here, but all over the world there were people like me sitting in offices, day after day after day, who did not fully appreciate the depth and the speed with which you were being engulfed by this unimaginable terror."

Dallaire would later show his anger at these kinds of half apologies from world leaders. "I blame the American leadership [for the lack of response], which includes the Pentagon, in projecting itself as the world's policeman one day and a recluse the next," he said.

The twentieth century was coming to a close, and still the world seemed no closer to stopping genocide than it had been at the start. While Rwanda exploded into violence that later subsided, a corner of Europe had also descended into bloody chaos. This conflict, in a region called the Balkans, would frustrate and humiliate world leaders—but it also provided a sliver of hope that genocide could, in fact, be stopped and its perpetrators brought to justice.

chapter six
the muslims of bosnia

in July 1996, Clea Koff stepped off an airplane in Bosnia and Herzegovina, a country in southeastern Europe, on a special mission. The cheerful young American was part of a team that had come to solve a terrible mystery. Just one year before, nearly eight thousand men and boys had been forced to leave the town of Srebrenica to walk across a war-torn region to the town of Tuzla. They had never arrived, and it was suspected that they had been executed as part of a campaign of genocide. Koff and the team were determined to find them and discover what had happened.

Forensic anthropologist Clea Koff led a team of scientists on a search for the truth about what happened to the Muslims in Bosnia in the 1990s.

Koff had studied forensic anthropology in the United States. She learned how to examine human remains to determine how people had died. It might appear to be a gruesome profession to some, but to Koff, it was part of a fascinating process of discovery. Ultimately, forensic anthropology uses science to arrive at truth.

Truth may be the most important weapon in the battle against genocide. Almost all perpetrators of genocide deny that a crime has occurred. They try to hide bodies or weapons (the Nazis destroyed many of the death camps themselves). Leaders often claim that the charges of genocide are lies told by political enemies or other countries seeking to gain an advantage over them. "Where are the bodies?" they ask. "Where is the proof of genocide?"

This was the case in Bosnia and Herzegovina (which is typically referred to as Bosnia) in the mid-1990s. After the fall of the Berlin Wall in 1990, many areas that had once been under the influence of the Soviet Union were rocked by political instability. The nation of Yugoslavia began to fall apart. In hindsight, this seems predictable. Yugoslavia actually consisted of a patchwork of ethnicities and religions that had been united under a strong and often repressive Communist government for more than forty years. The people, however, had memories, identities, and rivalries that stretched back for centuries.

Slovenia and Croatia declared independence, and war soon erupted between Croatia and neighboring Serbia. When Bosnia also tried to secede, the Serbian army invaded. The war was justified by the Serbs in terms of race and religion. The Serbs were Orthodox Christian, and they declared that they were coming to the aid of fellow Serbs living in Bosnia who were being abused by Muslim forces. Bosnia at the time was a mix of

Christians and Muslims (this area had been ruled for centuries by the Ottoman Empire), and the Serbs began to systematically empty villages of Muslims and destroy the mosques. Some observers of this process, which came to be called ethnic cleansing, accused the Serbs of committing genocide. This is a charge disputed vigorously then—and now—by the Serbs.

Deniers of Genocide

The legacy of genocide is so powerful—and the actual facts often so unbelievable—that many deny that genocide ever occurred. In 1993 a poll revealed that 22 percent, or one in five, of American adults answered that it was "possible" the Holocaust never occurred. While this may reflect an ignorance of history, some have actively sought to disprove that the Holocaust or other genocides ever happened in the first place. Some scholars have called these denials "the final stage of genocide."

There are many reasons that people deny genocide. It may be one more way of attacking a group. It could also be done to protect people who may have committed the crime. Or, because the crime of genocide is so enormous, a nation may refuse to acknowledge that it is part of its history. Turkey, for example, has denied for eighty years that genocide occurred against the Armenians. According to critics, Turkey has funded professors at American universities who support and advance the idea that no genocide occurred.

This map shows the location of Bosnia and Herzegovina, select cities, and neighboring countries.

Serbian forces used former Yugoslavian military equipment to attack Bosnia, which was defended by ill-equipped units. The Serbian forces surrounded the capital city, Sarajevo, and artillery in the surrounding hills battered the city's buildings. Snipers shot down civilians walking in the streets. Around the world, people reacted with disbelief and horror. Just hours from the comfortable capitals of Western Europe, people were killing one another with a savagery last seen in World War II.

"We Must Do Something"

Many Western leaders loudly expressed sympathy and resolved to act. Some in Europe called it a crisis that would allow Europe to assert itself as a united force on the world stage and bring peace to the region. Luxembourg's foreign minister, Jacques Poos, declared, "Now Europe's hour has come."

Nothing, however, seemed to actually affect events on the ground. The United States, now undisputedly the world's superpower, was reluctant to get involved in a bloody conflict that many believed was a nasty civil war based on centuries of divisions and hatred. All sides, they reasoned, were to blame. Politicians deplored the massacres, and editorial pages expressed outrage, but the killings, shootings, and ethnic cleansing continued.

Rumors began to circulate that the Serbs had created a number of camps for captured Muslims. Refugees described murders, starvation, and the abuse of women. In the summer of 1992, Western journalists gained access to the camps and

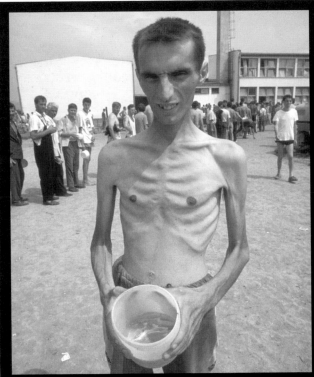

Prison camps in Bosnia were full of men that were tortured and starving to death.

questioned inmates and recently released prisoners. The stories—of tortures and executions—were terrible, but it was the images that would prove to be shocking. Listless prisoners stood behind barbed wire, their skin drawn tight over their ribs, shoulder blades, and cheekbones. The similarity between these images and those of the Nazi concentration camps at the end of World War II was unmistakable.

"The chilling reports from Bosnia evoke this century's greatest nightmare, Hitler's genocide against Jews, Gypsies and Slavs," wrote the *New York Times*. Public approval in the United States for air strikes jumped above 50 percent, and criticism of inaction grew intense. President George H. W. Bush, locked in a reelection battle against opponent Bill Clinton, pledged that all camps would be inspected. However, little else was done.

After Clinton defeated Bush in November 1992 and became president of the United States, supporters of Muslims in Bosnia hoped the new president would use American power to bring peace to the Balkans. They were soon disappointed. Though Clinton had constantly criticized Bush for doing too little in Bosnia, Clinton and his advisers were soon explaining why intervening in Bosnia was not feasible, reasonable, or a solution to the chaos there.

Elie Wiesel, as he had with Reagan earlier, made his opinion known to Clinton. "I have been in the former Yugoslavia last fall. I cannot sleep since what I have seen. As a Jew I am saying that. We must do something to stop the bloodshed in that country."

"Safe Area" Srebrenica

Still, no U.S. soldiers were sent to the region. Under the UN, however, several countries had sent forces to Bosnia. In one town, Srebrenica, about sixty thousand Muslim refugees had flowed into the city to escape the fighting. As Serb forces approached the city in March 1993, a French UN commander bluffed his way through Serb lines and saw the thousands of starving, sick people in Srebrenica. He immediately declared that the people were "under the protection of the UN." The Serb forces reluctantly halted. Just a month later, the UN declared that Srebrenica and 30 square miles (78 square kilometers) around it was a "safe area"—the first one in UN history. Srebrenica, however, seemed a bad choice to many. The city was deep in eastern Bosnia, surrounded by Serbian forces and within 10 miles (16 km) of the Serbian border.

Over the next few years, Srebrenica and two other "safe areas" in eastern Bosnia had a tenuous existence. The war had exhausted both the Serbs and the Bosnians, and there had been hope for a settlement. But it was clear that the Serbs wanted the eastern safe areas erased, and many Western diplomats, who saw the land as indefensible, secretly agreed.

UN forces, equipped with sky blue helmets and driving in white armored vehicles, tried to maintain some kind of authority. However, there was little question that they would be able to mount any kind of adequate defense against the larger Serb forces around them. Their only real deterrent was the North Atlantic Treaty Organization (NATO) warplanes based in nearby Western Europe. Yet even using these planes involved a complicated decision-making process that would not be fast enough to react to events on the ground. When Serbs became too aggressive around the safe areas, by shelling them for example, NATO warplanes conducted pinprick bombing attacks. When that happened, the Serbs retaliated by seizing UN soldiers as prisoners. To secure their release, the bombing attacks were called off.

In January 1995, a force of several hundred Dutch soldiers arrived in Srebrenica, commanded by Tom Karremans. By this time, the fighting in Bosnia appeared to have stabilized somewhat, with no town being captured by either army for almost two years. However, it appeared that Serbs were growing determined to take Srebrenica, and on July 6, 1995, they began their attack.

Hundreds of Muslims in the city, realizing that it was about to fall, fled into nearby woods. On July 10, with the Serbs about to enter the city, UN commander Bertrand Janvier authorized an air strike. Around the city, the Serb forces suddenly halted and the air strike was canceled. The next afternoon, however, NATO warplanes bombed Serb forces, though this ultimately did little damage to the Serbs. Serb soldiers angrily seized Dutch soldiers and threatened to kill them. This was enough to halt any more air strikes, and in the early evening, Srebrenica was captured by the Serbs.

Nightmare at Srebrenica

At first, it seemed that nothing bad would happen. The Serbian general Ratko Mladic assured the crowds of Muslim civilians that "those who want to leave, can leave. There is no need to be frightened." In front of camera crews, Mladic and his men passed out chocolates to Muslim children. More than fifty buses arrived in Srebrenica to deport Muslim civilians from the city. When he met with representatives of the town, Mladic demanded that all weapons be turned over to him. "I guarantee that all those who surrender their weapons will live," he said. "I need a clear answer so I can decide both as a man and as a commander."

As would be learned later, Mladic had already made up his

mind. When the loaded buses left the city, they were soon halted by Serbian soldiers. All men and boys aged twelve to seventy-seven were separated from the rest of the group, as the Serbs explained, to be questioned for war crimes.

Serb soldiers guard the deserted streets of Srebrenica after the Serb army took over the UN safe area in July 1995.

As this was going on, hundreds of Muslim men were wandering through the surrounding mountains and forests. Most hoped to somehow reach the safety of Muslim territory 40 miles (64 km) away, and they would rather risk the minefields and treacherous mountain terrain than Serb "mercy." Most of them were snared by Serbian patrols or lured out of hiding by Serbs wearing stolen blue UN helmets and riding in white UN vehicles.

As the buses ferried Muslim women and children out of Srebrenica, thousands of Muslim men, either from the city or captured nearby, were herded into open fields, empty warehouses, and factories. At a nearby Dutch base, Potocari, thousands of Muslim refugees gathered, hoping to be protected by the Dutch soldiers. Serbs demanded they be turned over to them, and the Dutch peacekeepers acquiesced.

Over the next few days, the staccato of machine-gun fire and the concussion of grenade blasts filled the area around Srebrenica. When asked, Serb commanders explained that Serb soldiers were celebrating their victory by firing into the air. Yet disturbing accounts were related from the first Muslim women and children to arrive in safe territory. They spoke of a blur of horrible images—of the men pulled from their families, of dead strewn along the road, of young women taken by Serb soldiers and never seen again. On July 14, a UN top official mentioned in a cable that "we are beginning to detect a short-fall in [the] number of persons expected to arrive in Tuzla. There is no further information on the status of the approximately 4,000 draft age males."

Uncovering a Crime

Almost one year after this message was sent, Clea Koff and a team of forensic anthropologists pulled up to a secluded spot located on a curve in a road near Cerska, just west of Srebrenica. By this time, as part of the peace agreement, U.S. forces were in Bosnia, and Koff's team was accompanied by a convoy of U.S. Army Humvees and Bradley armored vehicles. Koff thought it was the perfect place for a picnic, but she and the team were soon working on mapping the hundreds of empty shell casings strewn along the road. By the next day, they had uncovered a shallow trench filled with bodies, and within a week, they had uncovered 150.

The team moved on to other sites around Srebrenica. More bodies were uncovered. Koff, along with other teammates, speculated about how the boys and men had died. All had been hit at close range by a high-velocity weapon. Had they been shot on the edge of the pits and fallen in? Were they already in the pits when the shooting began? Some of the bodies were on their knees. Some were lying stretched out. This kind of language may sound cold and analytical, but it was critically important to the work that was being done—bringing the killers to justice.

Koff, who had worked in Rwanda, found herself thinking how similar it was to her work in Bosnia.

Forensic anthropologist William Haglund uncovers bodies in pits in Srebrenica.

The bodies could have been the same: again, their hands had been tied behind their backs; again, they were all males; again, there were a range of ages; again, they were wearing civilian clothes. I knew there were thousands of men missing from Srebrenica—we had only uncovered about two hundred by then. Just as in Rwanda, I sensed them on other fields, up other dirt tracks, an entire community—albeit just males—of dead all around us.

I felt anger toward people who deem murder an acceptable political policy. I felt the last of my naivete drain away as I uncovered more and more people shot while their hands were tied. And I felt two kinds of duty: one to the bodies—to identify them and allow them to incriminate their killers, the other to their relatives—to help return the remains to them.

But first the bodies had to tell their stories. A morgue was set up in a garment factory that was scarred with shell and bullet holes in the city of Kalesija. Each body was stored in a refrigerated area before it was taken, one at a time, to an X-ray machine. The X-ray revealed all pieces of metal—belt buckles, keys, jewelry—but also bullets or other metal fragments. Each projectile was then removed from the body and submitted to a technician to be analyzed as evidence.

All clothing was removed from the bodies, and the bones were reconstructed in their general anatomical position. By studying different parts of the bones, Koff was able to determine gender and age of the person and also examine signs of abuse—such as a bullet hole—to determine whether it had happened before or after the person had died.

As Koff performed this painstaking work, she also began to take in more of the countryside around her. She noticed posters of General Mladic in some towns, along with warnings to

A Bosnian Muslim man examines remains that were exhumed from a mass grave in an attempt to identify members of his family.

NATO troops that there would be no peace if Mladic was arrested. She also saw groups of women, calling themselves Women of Srebrenica, in demonstrations, weeping and holding up pictures of missing men.

As the morgue processed bodies and entered them into a computer database, Koff and her team also took stories from women who were seeking their loved ones. Koff noted that the most critical piece of information these women offered often turned out to be their sewing pattern. Because Srebrenica had been cut off from most of the world for so long, the women had frequently patched their families' clothing, each with a unique style of stitching. A repaired piece of clothing could be recognized by the woman who sewed it, and thus the bodies of family members could be identified.

Koff found herself torn between her job, which was to collect and analyze evidence, and the instinct to return something—even if it was just some stitching—to those who had lost someone. One day a fellow scientist showed her an unusual piece of evidence—a leg bone with a bullet lodged in it. Koff thought this was interesting, and then she laid out the rest of the bones. One of the bones in the hip was just fusing, a sign that the person had been under twenty-one years of age. Another bone revealed that he was even younger, between sixteen and eighteen. Though Koff had already examined hundreds of bodies strictly from a scientific perspective, this time an image formed in her mind—of a young man, perhaps no more than a boy, on the hillside at Cerska.

> I 'felt' the pain of the bullet entering his thigh just above the knee; I could sense his youth and the tragedy of it all and I thought of his family and what they were missing, and I thought of what one of the Women had said—how someone had told her they last saw her son getting on a bus with lots of other men and he was crying—and how that was the last she ever heard about him.

An International Court?

Because of the work of Koff and hundreds of others, the story of what had happened at Srebrenica began to emerge. Many Serbs shared the perspective that it was they who were the victims in the war. There may have been some isolated terrible incidents, they admitted, but ethnic cleansing and massacres were propaganda spread by Muslims and their supporters.

This argument became more difficult to support when

hundreds of bodies had been recovered, their hands tied behind their backs and all evidence indicating that they had been shot at close range. Ten years after the massacres at Srebrenica, this evidence would finally be used to bring justice.

Raphael Lemkin had hoped that a permanent court of some kind would be created to prosecute those who committed genocide. He also recognized that such a court would take some time to create. All nations cherish their sovereignty, and an international court, in concept, threatened that sovereignty. Instead, most genocides were dealt with by temporary courts set up in the country where the crimes themselves had taken place.

The Nuremberg trial of Nazi war criminals had been a critically important development for international law. Until then, it was extremely rare that individuals were held responsible for actions during wartime. Many of the Nazis themselves would argue that they had done nothing but follow orders—as all soldiers do. This defense, however, did not succeed. "Crimes against international law are committed by men and not by abstract entities, and only by punishing individuals who commit such crimes can the provisions of international law be enforced," ruled the court. Of the twenty-two Nazis who were tried, three were acquitted, twelve were sentenced to death, and seven to various prison terms.

Yet the Nuremberg trials had a number of critics. Some believed that the trials didn't represent justice; they were simply the victors imposing their will on the defeated. It was just another example of "might makes right." Others argued from a legal perspective. They wondered how the Nazis could be convicted for laws that didn't exist on an international level before World War II. Another criticism was that the procedure for convicting war criminals was more lax than in many countries. In most countries, the death penalty required the consent of all members on a jury. In some war trials, however, death sentences were imposed by margins as slim as 6–5.

Despite these criticisms, the Nuremberg trials set an important example. Those who committed certain actions such as genocide, no matter when they were committed, could be held personally responsible. It took more than forty years, however, before the example set by Nuremberg was enforced again. In 1993 the United Nations established a court at The Hague, Netherlands, to prosecute violations of international law committed in Bosnia and the surrounding countries since 1991. Among the crimes listed was genocide.

The court spent several years gathering the evidence necessary to list those responsible for alleged war crimes. More than 160 Serbs were indicted. However, even when they had been accused, other Serbs refused to give them over to appear before the tribunal, which they regarded as a foreign plot to harm Serbia. As of late 2005, the highest-ranking Serbs accused of crimes, including Ratko Mladic, remained at large.

However, a number of lower-ranking officers were arrested and tried for their crimes, and a large number received prison sentences. Just as important, the courts provided a public forum for an extensive and exhaustive search for the truth. Presenting evidence in courts requires high standards. Also, the defense has the opportunity to tell its side of the story—to explain what it believes happened. The defense can also question witnesses or refute evidence. In the end, a trial is an opportunity to give the world something that often remains elusive about genocide— the truth. And the truth is essential for those who committed acts of genocide and those who suffered from it. Only when the truth is established can justice be done, wrongs addressed, and any kind of reconciliation begun.

A trial also gives history the terrible but irrefutable details.

On July 17, 1995, according to a tape played in court, a Colonel Popovic called his commander to say that 1,200 captives had been shot to death.

"Hello, it's Popovic, boss," he said. "Everything has been brought to an end. That job is done. No problems. I am here at the place. Can I just take a little break, take a shower? Basically that all gets an A. The grade is an A."

Later that night, Popovic tried to reach his commander to report that another group had been executed. "Tell the general I finished the job. I was there on the spot," he said. "It was horrible, horrible."

Intervention in Kosovo

The Balkans would not stay quiet. Largely because of U.S. leadership, NATO had brokered a truce among the warring factions around Bosnia. The deal had many critics, and hatred and dissatisfaction persisted in the region, but it was also a true peace.

In the southern part of Serbia is Kosovo, a province that holds deep historical and cultural meaning for the Serbs. However, it also contains a sizable minority of Albanians. As with many groups in the Balkans, the Albanians desired their own state, in this case independent of Serbian rule. The peace deal in 1995, however, did not recognize a separate Albania, and a group of rebels, called the Kosovo Liberation Army (KLA) formed. The KLA was a tiny band of determined Albanian men. They began making small attacks against Serb forces. When Serb police officers were murdered, Serb forces under the direction of Slobodan Milosevic moved into the region. Milosevic was a familiar figure in Yugoslavian politics and had served as president of Serbia during the bloody wars of the early 1990s.

Each atrocity against the Serbs was met with violence against the Albanian population. In a bid to rout out and capture KLA members, the Serb forces set villages aflame and drove the population into the countryside.

The startling images of yet more destruction and refugees in the Balkans provoked a far deeper response from NATO than in the early 1990s, when NATO made many threats but failed to carry them out. For one, the Kosovo situation could inflame the entire region, including Greece, a member of NATO. And this time, world opinion had shifted. After seeing massacres in Rwanda and Srebrenica, people were far more willing to use force to stop genocide. It had seemed to work in 1995 when NATO finally used credible force against the Serbs.

In January 1999, a group of forty-five Albanians were executed by Serbs and left in a ravine. This time, an American named William Walker was on the scene within twenty-four hours. He saw the bodies and confirmed the massacre. A month later, U.S. and European diplomats sat down with Serbian representatives outside Paris. They said the Serbs had to withdraw and accept the presence of an international peace force that would monitor the region. The Serbs rejected the offer.

On March 24, 1999, NATO jets roared into the air and began dropping missiles and bombs on the Serb forces. The next day, President Clinton justified the attacks to a national television audience. He invoked the language of genocide.

> We've seen innocent people taken from their homes, forced to kneel in the dirt and sprayed with bullets; Kosovar men dragged from their families, fathers and sons together, lined up and shot in cold blood. We learned some of the same lessons in Bosnia just a few years ago. The world did not act early enough to stop that war, either. And let's not forget what happened—innocent people herded into concentration

camps, children gunned down by snipers on their way to school, soccer fields and parks turned into cemeteries; a quarter of a million people killed, not because of anything they have done, but because of who they were.

In the following weeks, even as NATO airpower carried out strikes, the Serbs went on a massive offensive. They flushed out every Albanian, sending them into headlong flight. More than 1.3 million Kosovars fled. The air strikes continued. After seventy-eight days, Milosevic, facing unrest among his troops and a collapse in support among Serbians, surrendered. More than 50,000 NATO troops entered Kosovo, and more than 1 million Kosovars returned to their homes to pick up the pieces and resume their lives.

At the beginning of 2006, Kosovo technically remained part

After returning home to their destroyed village in Kosovo, a family grieves the deaths of their relatives.

of Serbia, but it was effectively independent under a UN
administration. Since November 2005, Serbian and Kosovar
leaders have engaged in UN-sponsored negotiations to
determine the future of the province. That future, at this point,
is still very unclear.

Legacy of Failure

Despite the success of intervention in Kosovo, the international
community's legacy in Srebrenica, as well as in Rwanda,
Cambodia, and during the Holocaust, is largely one of failure.
"Srebrenica crystallized a truth understood only too late by the
United Nations and the world at large: that Bosnia was as much
a moral cause as a military conflict," the United Nations
secretary general, Kofi Annan, wrote in a 1999 report. "The
tragedy of Srebrenica will haunt our history forever."

In almost every case of genocide in the twentieth century,
world leaders have avoided taking the difficult steps necessary to
prevent or stop it. The pattern has been one of denial, excuses,
and then repeated apologies—after the atrocities have occurred.
Then there is an assurance of "never again." Samantha Power
called it "the world's most unfulfilled promise."

Several organizations appeared in the late 1990s dedicated
to educating the public about genocide, observing states that are
in danger of descending into genocide, and lobbying to halt
genocide where it has appeared. Genocide Watch, founded in
The Hague, Netherlands, in 1999, describes eight stages of
genocide. The first three stages involve the separation of a group
into distinct groups, what the organization calls an "us vs.
them" mentality. Then one group is identified as being unclean,
sinister, or destructive, which permits many average or

indifferent people to regard the group as something less than human.

The next two stages concern organization. Genocides never "just happen," they require an enormous amount of planning and coordination. Units must be armed with weapons and trained how to use them. Once these plans are in place, certain individuals take opportunities to whip up hatred against the other group. This can include formal laws to separate the group from the rest of society or a violent targeting of moderates who urge some kind of reconciliation.

In the sixth and seventh stages, the group is targeted for destruction. This can include the creation of death lists (as in Rwanda) or some kind of formal identification of the group (such as Jews being forced to wear yellow stars). This is often followed by a forced relocation or confinement to ghettos. Once the group has been isolated, identified, and an apparatus created to kill them, the extermination stage can occur.

The final stage of genocide, according to Genocide Watch, is denial. Bodies are buried or burned, and camps are dismantled. The perpetrators deny that genocide ever occurred. They say it was isolated, random violence, or they blame the victims for bringing the genocide on themselves.

By identifying how genocides occur, Genocide Watch and other groups can attempt to spot genocide before it occurs. This theoretically can allow other parties to take measures that prevent the genocide and thus save thousands or millions of lives. These measures include condemnation, economic sanctions, political pressure, and assurances that those who commit the genocide will ultimately be held responsible.

Many say that the new International Criminal Court will be the forum to ensure that perpetrators of genocide never get away with their crimes. This will provide an important lesson for the future: If you commit genocide, you will be unable to flee. Any nation that gives you refuge will come under international pressure. Eventually, your crimes will be exposed to the world and you will be punished.

As Kofi Annan put it, the court serves a vital function of justice. "People all over the world want to know that humanity can strike back. That whenever genocide, war crimes or other such violations are committed, there is a court before which the criminal can be held to account, a court that puts an end to a global culture of impunity."

There are many criticisms of the court, one of which is that the wheels of justice move so slowly that actually capturing suspected perpetrators of genocide and trying them is extremely difficult. The former presiding judge of the Yugoslavia war crimes tribunal, Gabrielle Kirk McDonald, once pointed out that it has traditionally been "easier to go to prison for killing one man than for killing 100,000."

A last resort to prevent genocide is the use of force, but this complicates the issue enormously. Once the decision to use force is made, matters often spin out of control. Bombs and bullets cannot be taken back. Combat always is marred by mistakes, and civilians may be injured or killed. And, of course, the soldiers sent into action become targets. If soldiers are killed or wounded, public support for the operation may collapse.

Still, if there is one lesson learned since the early 1990s, it is that force or the credible threat of force appears to be a necessary part of any strategy to prevent or stop genocide. Columnist Anne Applebaum noted, "Sanctions and embargoes have never really worked against mass murderers, and humanitarian military intervention does not target the people who deserve it most. Only by holding individuals accountable, will crimes against humanity be stopped. The perpetrators themselves need to be personally frightened."

The debacle in Bosnia and the role the United States had to play to secure peace convinced many people—especially Americans—that force is the only credible way to prevent genocide and the United States is the only nation that can pull it off. Unfortunately, the supporters of intervention have collided with the International Criminal Court. Since U.S. soldiers are stationed in places all over the world, many believe that U.S. soldiers could be accused of committing war crimes and tried at the court. Critics of the court say that these prosecutions will be inspired by American enemies who have a grudge or who want to limit American power. The United States, they argue, has a unique role in the world to guarantee security and stability. It was U.S. soldiers who saved Bosnia and Kosovo, they say, not the International Criminal Court.

How then, can genocide be prevented? At the beginning of this book, we discussed how people can view themselves as different from others—and how this can devolve into genocide. Some argue that the solution to this is to simply identify everybody as being part of the same group. Two individuals from Boston and New York may identify themselves as living in different cities, but ultimately they consider each other Americans. The French and Germans see one another commonly as Europeans. Why not, say some, rise above all groups and recognize that we are all people—all members of the same species? We are, they say, "citizens of the world." This view may help promote a more peaceful world, say critics, but it still doesn't get to the root of the challenge—preventing genocide before it happens and stopping it where it has.

chapter seven
the tribes of darfur, sudan

It is certain that the debate has not finished. The newspapers have been full of stories about another genocide—this one in Sudan, a giant country in Africa that lies just south of Egypt. BBC journalist Fergal Keane wrote, "More than two million people have been uprooted. Hundreds of thousands, nobody really knows how many, have been killed. Thousands of women have been raped."

For almost twenty years, Sudan has been torn by civil war between the central government and rebels in the southern region of the country. The central reason for the conflict is oil, which is concentrated in the south and is mostly controlled by rebel groups. In 2003, however, due largely to U.S. pressure, peace talks between the two groups made advances. They formed a tentative plan for a new government and an agreement on how to divide income from the oil. But just as this war appeared to be resolved, another conflict flared up in Sudan's western region—Darfur.

Darfur's inhabitants are usually one of two groups—farmers or nomads. The differences between the groups are mainly cultural. Also, the farmers tend to be more African and the nomads more Arab. Both, however, are mostly Muslim, and both have lived in the region for centuries. Casually observed, an outsider may find it difficult to tell them apart.

But over the past fifteen years, friction between these

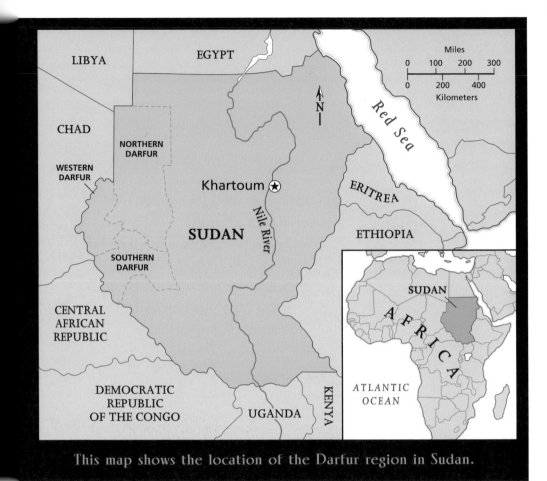

This map shows the location of the Darfur region in Sudan.

groups has increased. The nomads moved about the country with their herds, trampling the fields of farmers. Some farmers also own animals, which compete for food and space with the nomad's animals. Making everything worse, the population has grown and land has become scarce.

The farmers have also resented how the government has treated Darfur. The top local government positions seem to go only to candidates with Arab backgrounds. Also, the Khartoum regime appears to ignore Darfur, and no government money for roads, hospitals, or schools comes to the region. The tensions between these two groups escalated.

Another Genocide

The spark occurred in early 2003. After seeing the Khartoum government make peace with the southern rebels, some tribes in Darfur concluded that they could also use armed rebellion to make the government address their concerns. The Darfur rebels weren't taken seriously in Khartoum until they struck and overwhelmed an army post on April 25, 2003.

Shocked, the government moved quickly to crush the rebels, focusing on three Darfur tribes who were responsible for the protests. To carry out this task, the government gave weapons to local Arab militia groups and supported them with army soldiers and air force gunships. Among the most feared militia groups were nomads called Janjaweed (the word comes from Arabic—*jan* means "evil" in Arabic; *jawad* means "horse"). These forces began a vicious campaign against farming villages in Darfur.

Armed Janjaweed militiamen ride their horses in the western Darfur region of Sudan.

Without warning, villages were bombed and strafed by Sudanese airplanes. Then trucks loaded with soldiers, followed by columns of Janjaweed on camels and horses, surrounded and attacked the villages. In some cases, the villagers would flee and only lose their food, animals, and homes. In others the soldiers and Janjaweed slaughtered the men and boys and raped the women. After hours marked by screams, explosions, and bursts of gunfire, the Sudanese forces looted the villages and set the wood huts aflame.

The Janjaweed, their horses and camels loaded with furniture, rugs, and other loot, vanished back into the countryside. The trucks carrying soldiers drove off on the dirt roads, leaving behind smoking ruins and corpses, many of them thrown into wells to foul the water. Another village had been wiped out, and the process was sure to be repeated again. Flying over the region, observers could see the black smudges of destroyed villages scattered across the landscape.

Over the next year, details of what was happening in Darfur were gradually reported in the international press. Hundreds of thousands of refugees fled the region and told stories of villages bombed and the male inhabitants shot down before their eyes. The refugees, many of them starving, gathered in wretched camps. Human rights groups began labeling the Janjaweed action "ethnic cleansing," a term used earlier in Bosnia. The groups called for the government to allow humanitarian aid into the country and for the refugees be permitted to return to their homes safely.

On April 7, 2004, Kofi Annan brought up the crisis in a speech commemorating the tenth anniversary of the Rwandan genocide. "The international community cannot stand idle," he told his audience. "The risk of genocide remains frighteningly real." The government in Khartoum dismissed Annan's

A young boy grieves over all that remains of his house after the Janjaweed forces attacked his village in 2004.

comments, while rebel groups appealed for an international force to enforce peace in the country. Still, however, the atrocities kept occurring.

As the criticism of the Khartoum government grew, the government insisted that the stories of rapes and murders were exaggerated, the result of undisciplined soldiers in wartime, or simply a local tribal conflict. When negative news continued to be reported, however, the government promised it would halt and disarm the Janjaweed.

But the reports only grew worse. On July 30, 2004, the UN Security Council passed a resolution that threatened to consider sanctions if the Janjaweed were not curtailed. On September 9, 2004, U.S. secretary of state Colin Powell told the Senate Foreign Relations Committee that "genocide has been committed in

Darfur and that the government of Sudan and the Janjaweed bear responsibility—and genocide may still be occurring." The U.S. State Department reported on the same day that 1.2 million people have been forced to flee from their homes and that 405 villages had been destroyed.

Darfurian survivors gathered in camps, many exhausted and traumatized, and humanitarian groups did what they could to help them. The Paris-based group Doctors Without Borders sent medicine and doctors to the region. Dr. Jerry Ehrlich, a sixty-nine-year-old pediatrician from New Jersey, was already a veteran of several humanitarian missions. He had first volunteered his services to the organization in 1991 after reading newspaper stories about Kurds freezing in Kurdistan after the Gulf War. Over

This is one of many refugee camps in Chad, a neighboring country, where more than 150,000 Sudanese refugees were received.

the next fourteen years, Ehrlich spent time treating displaced persons and refugees in Sri Lanka, Haiti, and central Asia. In 2004 Ehrlich arrived in Nyala, a small town in southern Darfur.

Every day he and another doctor were driven several miles to a camp for displaced persons. As the truck bounced along the sandy track, he quietly noticed that more and more people were crowding into the camp. The fields of straw and wood huts, with plastic tarps thrown across the tops to ward off rain, were growing larger. At Kalma, the camp where Ehrlich spent most of his time, the population was forty-five thousand. When he left two months later, he estimated it had risen to seventy-five thousand.

The region had become a humanitarian crisis. Ehrlich saw hundreds of patients every day. Most of them, Ehrlich said, were either traumatized from what they had seen, malnourished from lack of food, or exhausted after fleeing dozens of miles. The agony was not just physical, he recalled. "The mothers, you look at their faces and you know they have a problem," he said. "It's post-traumatic stress disorder. They had seen their husbands beaten, or killed in front of them. Many of them were victims of gang rape."

Many of the children hadn't eaten well for weeks or months, said Ehrlich, making them especially vulnerable to diseases. A measles epidemic killed more than one in four children in the camp. Each week, remembered Erhlich, a humanitarian worker would go to a nearby cemetery to count the lengthening rows of graves.

While Ehrlich spent most of his time treating children, he gave out more than just advice and medicine. He had also brought to Darfur twenty-five boxes of crayons and four hundred pieces of construction paper. He gave some of his young patients crayons, sheets of paper, and told them to "have fun"—draw whatever they wanted to.

Ehrlich said he wanted the drawings partly as a memento of his time in Darfur and partly to help the children entertain themselves. "The kids sat in the hospital, sat in the camps," he recalled. "And they had nothing to do."

Dr. Jerry Ehrlich poses with a refugee child and her drawing.

Many of the children came back days or even weeks later to give Ehrlich their drawings. He thanked them and gave them either a hug or a handshake. Then, knowing that the images could be confiscated by the Sudanese authorities, he quickly stashed them in his bag. Later, back in his dormitory, he glanced at them before storing them safely between the pages of a Sunday *New York Times*.

When Ehrlich left Sudan at the end of July, he carried 167 drawings with him. Back home in New Jersey, where he finally had time to examine the drawings closely, he saw horrible images through the children's eyes—of burning huts, gun-wielding soldiers, and villagers being shot. "What can I tell you?" he said when asked how the drawings made him feel. "You could cry."

Ehrlich was aware of drawings made by Jewish children during the Holocaust that depicted similar violent images. The Holocaust drawings, which have been preserved, had impressed Ehrlich enormously. To him, they were vital historical documents and indisputable evidence of the atrocities that had occurred. He felt that the Darfur drawings could serve a similar purpose.

"It was proof that this was happening," he said. "Here you have some innocent kids, and this is what this child is drawing. Here you have a child's view of what's going on—through his eyes, through his mind."

This, he said, presented an opportunity. "I knew when I left Darfur I was not going to walk away without attempting to create public awareness," he said. "When I looked at those pictures, I knew I had to do something. I had to get them exhibited, viewed."

Through the help of a church, the drawings were mounted in an exhibit in Philadelphia in December 2004. After the show, which drew considerable local media and public interest ("The church was packed to the gills," remembered Ehrlich), the drawings were sent on tour, where they have been shown in dozens of shows to raise consciousness of what was happening in Darfur. Ehrlich often went to give talks on what he had seen.

At these talks, which he continues to do, Ehrlich meets many people who are determined to do something about the situation, but Ehrlich also feels some disappointment. His

These are two of the disturbing images that were created by Sudanese children who had witnessed the genocide in Darfur. The drawing at the top shows airplanes bombing burning houses and dead bodies. In the drawing to the right, notice the small child toward the top, caught between gunfire.

audience is often disturbed and shocked by what he says—which to him is not necessarily a good thing. "The awareness isn't there," he said. "If you could end this conflict a month earlier, you have no idea how many lives could be saved."

Another person who felt impelled to do something about Darfur was a teenage high school student from northern New Jersey. Arielle Wisotsky was visiting the Holocaust Memorial Museum with her mother in Washington, D.C. As she was exiting the main exhibit on the Holocaust, she noticed a poster and several flyers that spoke of a new genocide—in Darfur.

"I was kind of shocked—I had never heard about it," the seventeen-year-old said. "And it's genocide, and I was kind of surprised that no one really knows about it."

Wisotsky, whose grandmother had survived the Holocaust, pondered ways to help the situation. "I knew I wanted to help, but I didn't know how," she said. The obvious plan seemed to raise money somehow and donate it. "But I wanted to do more."

Like Ehrlich, Wisotsky believed that a large part of the problem was the lack of recognition. In fall 2005, she and two friends founded a nonprofit organization called Help Darfur Now. She printed flyers and sent them to family, friends, and members of the surrounding community.

Wisotsky participated in a march with other Darfur groups in Morristown, New Jersey. She has written to members of Congress, asking for meetings on the issue, and planned a school assembly. The group has raised more than $25,000, and in February 2006, presented a check to Doctors Without Borders for $15,000. The organization has expanded to include twenty-five satellite chapters (other middle and high school students in various parts of the United States have opened chapters of Help Darfur Now).

"I feel that it's working," she said. "Not a lot of people at my school knew about it; now they do. It feels good to be helping."

Getting Away with Murder

At the end of 2005, the genocide in Darfur continued. A seven-thousand-member force from a group of African nations—called the African Union—were sent to the region, but they lacked the numbers or equipment to alter the situation on the ground. In December 2005, the U.S. Congress rejected a last-minute plea from U.S. secretary of state Condoleezza Rice to appropriate $50 million to support the group. While the U.S. government has used extremely strong language to describe the events in Sudan, it didn't appear willing to do anything of true consequence—such as send in ground troops (this was also unlikely because of the conflict in Iraq).

On December 13, 2005, the Sudan government barred international investigators from entering the country to collect

A rebel soldier observes the remains of a body that was left unburied in order to preserve some evidence of the atrocities committed by the Janjaweed.

evidence on alleged war crimes. The presence of the International Criminal Court, insisted Sudanese officials, is unnecessary. "We have the national law authority," Sudanese minister of justice Muhammad Ali al-Mardi told the BBC. "The government is willing and able to try these cases."

At the United Nations, however, the mood was less confident. The humanitarian chief, Jan Egeland, has said that rapes, killings, and forced displacements were still occurring. In addition, the situation has become so dangerous that organizations may be forced to withdraw. And others see the situation in Sudan as already another failure—a name that can be added to a terrible list of atrocities that no one had the power or the resolve to stop.

"For all the epic quality of this tragedy, it feels like a very old script. We have been here before," wrote BBC journalist Fergal Keane, listing the various phrases that world leaders use to describe genocide. Besides "never again," he says, there is "we must learn the lessons." With growing disgust, Keane wrote a speech typical of public statements made by world leaders today. "'We must learn the lessons of the Holocaust, or of Cambodia, or of Bosnia, or of Rwanda . . . and make sure that things like this . . .' and you know how this sentence ends . . . 'things like this never happen again.'"

Bill Schulz, executive director of Amnesty International USA in New York, was far more angry. "How far have we really come [since the genocide in Rwanda]?" he asked. "The Sudanese government has been emboldened by international inaction. They think they can get away with murder, and frankly there's every reason to believe they are right."

chapter eight
survivors and witnesses

In winter 1945, in the last months of World War II, the camp at Auschwitz was liberated by advancing Russian armies. One of the inmates, a young man named Viktor Frankl, had been in the camp for more than a year. He had been sustained on a meager diet that left him weakened and half-starved. He had been the victim of beatings, had been worked to exhaustion, and had seen numerous acts of savagery and murder. Finally, a white flag fluttered over the camp, and the gates were left open.

Frankl and his fellow prisoners, most of whom were weak from lack of food, shuffled out beyond the barbed-wire fences for the first time. Frankl almost ducked when he saw the guards, recalling how they used to lash out with clubs and whips as the prisoners walked by. This time, however, the guards had quickly changed into civilian clothes and were passing out cigarettes to the prisoners—who could still not grasp that they were free.

In the next few months, the former prisoners began to walk in the countryside around the camp. One day, they saw a meadow full of flowers. "We realized that they were there, but we had no feelings about them. The first spark of joy came when we saw a rooster with a tail of multicolored feathers. But it remained only a spark; we did not yet belong to this world."

Many of those who survive genocide are in a separate world. Everything that they have known has been destroyed—

family, community, culture. And it is not just those directly affected by genocide who may feel this, but anyone who lived through it or near it. A British historian, Alfred Leslie Rowse, expressed this bitterness in 1979: "This filthy twentieth century. I hate its guts."

The Armenian community, shattered after the genocide, recovered and began a relentless campaign to win recognition and justice for what had happened. Armenian communities erected monuments to the genocide around the world, and today more than 130 memorials exist in twenty-five countries. Recognition has come slowly. In 1998 the French National Assembly formally called the massacre of the Armenians *genocide*. In the United States, the House of Representatives passed a similar declaration, but it was opposed by President Bill Clinton.

In 2005 Armenians visited a memorial in Yerevan, Germany, to the genocide victims to recognize the ninetieth anniversary of the mass killings.

Today, the U.S. government still officially refers to the genocide as a "tragedy."

The opposition to calling it a genocide reflects the importance of modern U.S. relations with Turkey, as well as the Turkish insistence that no more than 300,000 Armenians died and that the massacres did not constitute a genocide. "This subject cannot be tackled without negotiating a minefield of claim, counter-claim and fury," wrote the British newspaper the *Guardian*.

The Turkish position has been unchanged since the 1920s, and the Turkish government has gone to passionate lengths to defend it. In December 2005, the Turkish novelist Orhan Pamuk appeared in a Turkish court because he had been charged with "public denigration of Turkish identity." This occurred after Pamuk told a Swiss magazine during an interview that "30,000 Kurds and a million Armenians were killed in these lands and almost nobody but me dares to talk about."

Perhaps because of this silence about the past, the Turkish government today seems to be unable to escape its consequences. Turkey is eager to join the European Union (EU), but some EU representatives say this is impossible until Turkey fully admits to the Armenian genocide.

Germany's modern image is inextricably wound up in the Holocaust. Although the country has become a democracy and is considered a stalwart member of NATO, virtually every action is interpreted through the prism of genocide. On the sixtieth anniversary of the liberation of Auschwitz, a German newspaper wrote that "it is still true that nothing moves this country more than the time of its deepest shame," and that tens of thousands of Germans were responsible for the murder of millions "is beyond anybody's understanding and therefore beyond any explanation."

"All Germans who seriously think about themselves and their country will continue to be haunted by this," the paper stated.

Loung Ung, the child in Cambodia, ended up living in the United States, though she could never forget what she experienced. Leaving behind three siblings in Cambodia, she and her older brother had fled to a refugee camp in Thailand, where she lived for five months. They later spent two months on a houseboat in Vietnam.

Cambodian survivor and author Loung Ung

Her older brother, who had become the leader of the family now that their parents were dead, decided that she was scrappy and intelligent enough to survive in a new country. When an opportunity for both of them came to immigrate to the United States (through a program sponsored by the U.S. Conference of Catholic Bishops and Holy Family Church in Burlington, Vermont), her brother chose Ung to go. Ung settled with a family in Vermont, where she had to learn that the fireworks on the Fourth of July were not real missiles or bombs, and that she didn't have to hoard food under her bed. After growing up in the United States, Ung eventually returned to visit Cambodia and reunite with her sister. Ung titled her memoir about her life after leaving Cambodia *Lucky Child*.

In the meantime, some measure of justice finally appeared in Cambodia, when a UN tribunal began finding and prosecuting the individuals who participated in the Cambodian genocide. In 2003 a seventy-two-year-old ex–Khmer Rouge officer told the Associated Press that there was "no more doubt left" that his regime had committed genocide. Khieu Samphan was one of the few top Khmer Rouge officers still alive, and he faced an indictment from a UN tribunal. He insisted he was innocent, but he also acknowledged, "Everything has to go the trial's way now, and there's no other way," he said. Khieu Samphan is the only Khmer Rouge officer to face justice. Pol Pot, responsible for the murder of millions, died in his bed of a heart attack in 1998.

Since the genocides of the 1990s, emotions remain raw and many of the criminals responsible remain at large. Some say that unless the genocides are effectively dealt with, there will only be more genocides in the future. This is because genocide does not disappear into the era in which it is perpetrated. It forms a chain that links the past to the present and the future. Generations are raised on the tales of genocide. Resentment is nurtured and fanned, observed writer John Heidenrich. Descendants seek justice and vengeance.

Nazi Hunter

Simon Wiesenthal was born in 1908 in what is now Ukraine.
He somehow managed to survive incarceration in more than
ten concentration camps, including Auschwitz and
Buchenwald, though eighty-nine of his relatives were killed in
the Holocaust. With a phenomenal memory and a passion that
some described as obsessive, Wiesenthal began a lifelong hunt
to find the individuals who had participated in the Holocaust,
capture them, and bring them to trial. This was not easy.
Many Nazis had fled to South America and were living under
new identities.

Nazi hunter Simon
Wiesenthal helped
bring more than one
thousand Nazi war
criminals to justice.

Working out of a cramped office in Vienna, Austria, with one or two assistants, Wiesenthal helped uncover Holocaust mastermind Adolf Eichmann in Argentina, who was later wrapped in a carpet and smuggled out of the country by Israeli agents to stand trial in Israel. Eichmann was found guilty and executed. Wiesenthal helped to find Franz Stangl, the commandant of death camps at Treblinka and Sobibor, and SS officer Josef Schwammberger, who was tried in a German court and sentenced to life in prison. Wiesenthal made many enemies, and his office was firebombed by neo-Nazis, but his impact was indisputable. Wiesenthal himself claimed he helped bring more than one thousand Nazis to justice.

Wiesenthal was later asked why he didn't resume his career in architecture after the war. He answered, "When we come to the other world and meet the millions of Jews who died in the camps and they ask us, 'What have you done?' there will be many answers. You will say, 'I became a jeweler.' Another will say, 'I smuggled coffee and American cigarettes.' Still another will say, 'I built houses,' but I will say, 'I didn't forget you.'"

Wiesenthal died in September 2005 at the age of ninety-six. The newspaper the *Guardian* noted in its obituary that Wiesenthal had done more than simply track down and catch criminals. "Arguably his most important legacy was to convince a growing mass of public opinion that war crimes trials are an essential tool in healing the wounds of genocide."

Portraits of Bosnian Muslims who were victims of the 1995 Srebrenica massacre were displayed in a room in the Bosnian town of Tuzla where survivors and dignitaries gathered in 2005 to attend a ceremony marking the tenth anniversary of the massacre.

Slobodan Milosevic, the leader of Serbia through the 1990s, was arrested and brought before the International Criminal Court, where he was accused of masterminding genocide in Bosnia. At The Hague, Milosevic denounced the court as illegal, accused NATO of war crimes, and said Srebrenica was a plot hatched by French and Bosnian spies to make the world hate Serbia. When Milosevic grew too loud, the judge turned off his microphone. Starting in 2002, witness after witness described shootings, rapes, and destruction at the hands of Milosevic's forces. The trial never finished. On March 11, 2006, Milosevic died of a heart attack in his cell, eluding the court's final judgment.

In Rwanda the violence left more than 100,000 orphans, all of them growing up with the knowledge that their parents have been murdered. "Can any Western country be so certain that Africa will remain so utterly unimportant over the next several decades that the West can, at present, willfully ignore how genocide shapes Africa's adults?" asked Heidenrich.

The genocide in Rwanda left tens of thousands of orphans in camps across the country.

Paul Rusesabagina and the courage he showed during the Rwanda genocide became the subject of a film in 2004—*Hotel Rwanda*. The film and media attention has made Rusesabagina into something of a celebrity. He has won numerous awards, including the National Civil Rights Museum's National Freedom Award and the International Freedom Award. Through it all, Rusesabagina has maintained a sense of humor. When he was asked how true to life *Hotel Rwanda* was, he said,

> *Well, you can say that 90 percent of the movie is the reality of what took place at the Milles Collines hotel in 1994. Let's say 10 percent is just in hints of the film. . . . There are places, for instance, romantic times when you see Paul and his wife on the roof, enjoying wine. That good time, I didn't have it. I could go and see my wife and children late in the night, around two, around one, around four in the night, but that good time, I didn't have it.*

Though he and his wife have seen the film many times, he says he still won't show it to anyone else in Rwanda. The images remain too raw. "I've been always trying to show it, the copy I have, but sometimes when I feel like showing it, it takes me time. Two hours, three hours, and I change my mind," he said. "It is not easy to show the children. Their parents died in such an atrocity."

The Rwandan government has implemented some reform in recognition of the genocide. On January 1, 2006, the nation's twelve provinces were consolidated into five. One of the reasons for the change was that it would weaken the central authority. That way, some reasoned, a genocide would be more difficult to organize in the future. Another reason is that the new provinces are more ethnically diverse. It was hoped that this would help the country overcome its ethnic divisions.

Elie Wiesel, who wrote in *Night* that the horrors of Auschwitz had consumed his faith forever, settled in France and then New York. His writings on the Holocaust made him an internationally respected figure, a position he continues to use

Holocaust survivor and Nobel Peace Prize winner Elie Wiesel stands between two candles during a Holocaust Commemoration Ceremony at the World Economic Forum in Davos, Switzerland, in 2005.

to speak against intolerance, injustice, and oppression. In 1986 Wiesel was awarded the Nobel Peace Prize.

At the Nobel Prize ceremony, Wiesel opened with these words: "Words of gratitude. First to our common Creator. This is what the Jewish tradition commands us to do. At special occasions, one is duty-bound to recite the following prayer: 'Barukh atah adonai, eloheinu melech ha'olam, shehekhyanu vekiymanu vehigianu lazman hazeh.'—'Blessed be Thou for having sustained us until this day.'"

Wiesel continued, speaking first of his experience and then describing what it meant:

I remember: it happened yesterday, or eternities ago. A young Jewish boy discovered the Kingdom of Night. I remember his bewilderment, I remember his anguish. It all happened so fast. The ghetto. The deportation. The sealed cattle car. The fiery altar upon which the history of our people and the future of mankind were meant to be sacrificed.

I remember he asked his father: "Can this be true? This is the twentieth century, not the Middle Ages. Who would allow such crimes to be committed? How could the world remain silent?"

And now the boy is turning to me. "Tell me," he asks, "what have you done with my future, what have you done with your life?" And I tell him that I have tried. That I have tried to keep memory alive, that I have tried to fight those who would forget. Because if we forget, we are guilty, we are accomplices.

And then I explain to him how naïve we were, that the world did know and remained silent. And that is why I swore never to be silent whenever wherever human beings endure suffering and humiliation. We must take sides. Neutrality helps the oppressor, never the victim. Silence encourages the tormentor, never the tormented. Sometimes we must interfere. When human lives are endangered, when human dignity is in jeopardy, national borders and sensitivities become irrelevant. Wherever men and women are persecuted because of their race, religion, or political views, that place must—at that moment—become the center of the universe.

—Elie Wiesel

timeline

armenian genocide

1914, August	World War I begins.
1915, April	Forced removal of Armenians begins.
1915, April–May	Turkish government begins to deport Armenians from their villages, either massacring the inhabitants or forcing them to flee.
1915, May 24	France, Great Britain, and Russia warn Turkey that members of the Turkish government will be held responsible for crimes against Armenians.
1915, June–December	Whole populations of Armenians are deported and either shot or forced onto death marches.
1916–1918	Genocide continues in various forms, with surviving Armenians deported, killed, or forced to convert to Islam.
1918, November	World War I ends.
1921	Talaat is assassinated in Berlin by Soghomon Tehlirian.

genocide of european jews

1933, January 30	Hitler is appointed chancellor of Germany.
1933, February 27	Reichstag is burned. Nazis seize emergency powers.
1939, September 1	Germany invades Poland. World War II begins.

1941, June 22	Germany invades the Soviet Union. Large Jewish populations of eastern Europe fall under Nazi control. *Einsatzgruppen* begin massacring Jews.
1941, December	Chelmno extermination camp opens.
1942, March–June	Belzec and Sobibor death camps are opened. Auschwitz extermination and work camps are established.
1942–1944	Nazis pursue European Jews relentlessly, killing millions.
1945, May 7	Germany surrenders unconditionally. World War II ends in Europe.
1945, November 22	Nuremberg trials of Nazi war criminals begin.
1948, December 8	Text declaring genocide a crime is adopted by representatives of the United Nations.

Cambodia genocide

1975	The Khmer Rouge capture the Cambodian capital city, Phnom Penh, and begin to force the city's population into the countryside.
1975–1978	Under the rule of Khmer Rouge, between 1.7 and 2.5 million Cambodians are murdered (out of a population of 8 million).
1979, January	Vietnam invades Cambodia and captures Phnom Penh, ending Khmer Rouge rule.

bosnia genocide

1991	Yugoslavia breaks apart into warring independent nations. Croatia, Slovenia, and Bosnia and Herzegovina declare independence. Ethnic groups within each nation begin fighting.

1992	Serbian forces begin a campaign of ethnic cleansing in Bosnia.
1992–1995	The Bosnian city of Sarajevo is shelled and exposed to sniper and mortar fire during a Serbian siege.
1993, April–May	Several UN safe areas are established for Bosnian Muslims.
1995, July 11	Srebrenica falls to Serbian forces. In the following weeks, thousands of Muslim men and boys are massacred.
1995, August–September	NATO air strikes pound Serb positions.
1995, November 21	Serbs, Croats, and Bosnians agree to a peace deal. A treaty is signed on December 14 in Paris.

rwanda genocide

1994, April 6	A plane carrying Rwandan president Habyarimana and Burundian president Cyprien Ntaryamira is shot down as it approaches Kigali International Airport.
1994, April 7	Hutu military units and armed gangs begin to round up and murder Tutsi and moderate Hutu. Ten Belgian soldiers are tortured and killed.
1994, April 8	The Rwandan Patriotic Front (RPF) launches an attack to stop the murders.
1994, April 8–10	Intensity of the attacks grows as thousands are murdered.
1994, April 9–10	France and Belgium evacuate their citizens.
1994, April 15	Thousands who gathered for refuge at the church of Nyarubuye are killed.

1994, April 21	The UN withdraws most of its forces. International groups estimate that hundreds of thousands of Tutsi Rwandans have been killed.
1994, May 17	The UN claims that "acts of genocide" may have occurred in Rwanda.
1994, mid-May	The International Red Cross believes more than five hundred thousand Rwandans have been slaughtered.
1998, March 25	In a speech in Kigali, President Clinton apologizes for lack of action during Rwandan genocide.

kosovo

1996–1997	Bombings and clashes between Serbian police and the separatist group, Kosovo Liberation Army (KLA), intensify.
1998, January–March	Serb police forces carry out several operations in Kosovo.
1998, September	Serb forces begin to empty Kosovo villages. NATO prepares to launch air strikes. Several efforts are made to broker a peace.
1999, March	After peace talks among Serbs and Kosovars fail, Serbian forces invade Kosovo and begin ethnic cleansing of the region.
1999, March 24	NATO air strikes begin. Thousands of Kosovar refugees flee south.
1999, April	NATO air strikes continue, and the refugee situation becomes a crisis as hundreds of thousands are displaced.
1999, May	Slobodan Milosevic is indicted for crimes against humanity in Kosovo, charges of genocide in Bosnia, and more.

1999, June	Serbian forces begin to withdraw from Kosovo.
1999, June 10	NATO halts the bombing campaign, and Russian and NATO forces enter Kosovo two days later.
2006, March 11	Slobodan Milosevic dies under mysterious circumstances after five years in prison while awaiting the conclusion of his trial.

darfur genocide

2004, January	The Sudanese army moves into the western region of Darfur to put down a rebellion. The action forces hundreds of thousands to flee to neighboring Chad.
2004, March	A UN official says pro-government Arab Janjaweed militias are responsible for systematically destroying villages and murdering the inhabitants in Darfur..
2004, April–June	International criticism of Sudan and the situation in Darfur grows.
2004, September	U.S. secretary of state Colin Powell describes the Darfur killings as genocide.
2005, January	UN report accuses the Sudanese government and militias of systematic abuses in Darfur but does not call the violence genocide.
2006 March-April	Sudan refuses entry to UN Emergency Relief Coordinator Jan Egeland, who planned to visit the region to assess the humanitarian situation.
2006 March	The International Organization for Migration reports that violence in Darfur is "as bad as ever."

for further information

books

Bagdasarian, Adam. *Forgotten Fire.* New York: Dell Laurel-Leaf, 2002.

Bauer, Yehuda. *A History of the Holocaust.* Danbury, CT: Franklin Watts, 2002.

Fisanick, Christina. *Rwanda Genocide.* San Diego: Greenhaven Press, 2004.

Moore, Lisa. *Elie Wiesel: Surviving the Holocaust, Speaking Out about Genocide.* Berkeley Heights, NJ: Enslow Publishers, 2005.

Sacco, Joe. *Safe Area Gorazde: The War in Eastern Bosnia 1992–1995.* New York: Fantagraphic Books, 2002.

movies & documentaries

Auschwitz: Inside the Nazi State. BBC, 2005.

Ghosts of Rwanda. Paramount Home Video, 2005.

The Killing Fields. Warner Studios, 2001.

Night and Fog. Criterion Collection, 1955.

The Pianist. Universal Studios, 2003.

Schindler's List. Universal Studios, 1993.

Shoah: An Oral History of the Holocaust. New Yorker Video, 2003.

Sometimes in April. Warner Home Video, 2005.

websites

Armenian National Institute
   http://www.armenian-genocide.org/

Cambodia Genocide: Memories from Tuol Sleng Prison
   http://www.fathom.com/feature/35706/

Genocide: Resources for Teaching and Research
   http://www.people.memphis.edu/~genocide/hellox.htmlx

"The Holocaust Martyrs' and Heroes' Remembrance Authority." *Yad Vashem.*
   http://www.yadvashem.org/

PBS. "America and the Holocaust." *American Experience.*
   http://www.pbs.org/wgbh/amex/holocaust/index.html

PBS. "The Triumph of Evil: How the West Ignored Warnings of the 1994 Rwanda Genocide and Turned Its Back on the Victims." *Frontline*. http://www.pbs.org/wgbh/pages/frontline/shows/evil/

United States Holocaust Memorial Museum
http://www.ushmm.org/

Yale University Cambodian Genocide Program
http://www.yale.edu/cgp/

iPod broadcast

The U.S. Holocaust Memorial Museum has created a podcast called "Voices on Genocide Prevention." It presents the views of human rights activists, scholars, journalists, and government officials on genocide. To download the podcast, visit http://www.ushmm.org/conscience/podcasts/.

bibliography

Bard, Mitchell, ed. *The Complete History of the Holocaust*. San Diego: Greenhaven Press, 2001.

Browning, Christopher. *Ordinary Men: Reserve Police Battalion 101 and the Final Solution in Poland*. New York: HarperCollins, 1992.

———. *The Origins of the Final Solution*. Lincoln: University of Nebraska Press; Jerusalem: Yad Vashem, 2004.

Charny, Israel W., ed. *Encyclopedia of Genocide*. Santa Barbara, CA: ABC-CLIO, 1999.

Craig, Gordon A. *The Germans*. New York: G. P. Putnam's Sons, Inc., 1991.

Fleck, Dieter. *The Handbook of Humanitarian Law in Armed Conflicts*. New York: Oxford University Press, 1995.

Gilbert, Martin. *The Holocaust: A History of the Jews of Europe during the Second World War*. New York: Henry Holt & Company, 1985.

Gourevitch, Philip. *We Wish to Inform You that Tomorrow We Will Be Killed with Our Families: Stories from Rwanda*. New York: Picador, 1998.

Graber, G. S. *Caravans to Oblivion: The Armenian Genocide 1915*. New York: John Wiley and Sons, Inc., 1996.

Heidenrich, John G. *How to Prevent Genocide: A Guide for Policymakers, Scholars, and the Concerned Citizen*. Westport, CT: Praeger Publishers, 2001.

Keane, Fergal. *Season of Blood: A Rwandan Journey.* London: Penguin Books, 1995.

Kiernan, Ben. *The Pol Pot Regime: Race, Power, and Genocide under the Khmer Rouge, 1975–1979.* New Haven, CT: Yale University Press, 1996.

Koff, Clea. *The Bone Woman: A Forensic Anthropologist's Search for Truth in the Mass Graves of Rwanda, Bosnia, Croatia, and Kosovo.* New York: Random House, 2004.

Lanzmann, Claude. *Shoah: An Oral History of the Holocaust.* New York: Random House, 1985.

McCuen, Marnie J. *The Genocide Reader: The Politics of Ethnicity and Extermination.* Hudson, WI: Gary E. McCuen Publications, 2000.

Miller, Donald E., and Lorna Touryan. *Survivors: An Oral History of the Armenian Genocide.* Berkeley: University of California Press, 1993.

Power, Samantha. *"A Problem from Hell": America and the Age of Genocide.* New York: Basic Books, 2002.

Pran, Dith. *Children of Cambodia's Killing Fields.* New Haven, CT: Yale University Press, 1997.

Rhodes, Richard. *Masters of Death: The SS Einsatzgruppen and the Invention of the Holocaust.* New York: Alfred Knopf, 2002.

Rohde, David. *Endgame: The Betrayal and Fall of Srebrenica, Europe's Worst Massacre Since World War II.* Boulder, CO: Westview Press, 1998.

Rosenbaum, Alan. *Is the Holocaust Unique?* Boulder, CO: Westview Press, 2001.

Rummel, Rudolph. *Death by Government.* New Brunswick, NJ: Transaction Publishers, 1994.

Sells, Michael. *The Bridge Betrayed: Religion and Genocide in Bosnia.* Berkeley: University of California Press, 1996.

Sereny, Gitta. *Into That Darkness: An Examination of Conscience.* New York: Vintage Books, 1974.

Totten, Samuel, William S. Parsons, and Israel W. Charny, eds. *Century of Genocide: Eyewitness Accounts and Critical Views.* New York: Garland Publishers Inc., 1997.

Ung, Loung. *First They Killed My Father: A Daughter of Cambodia Remembers.* New York: HarperCollins, 2000.

Wiesel, Elie. *Night.* New York: Bantam Books, 1982.

a note on sources

I am deeply indebted to a number of sources for the research and writing of this book. The first is Samantha Power's award-winning "A Problem from Hell," which I borrowed from extensively for my sketches of Raphael Lemkin and his lonely crusade to have genocide recognized as an international crime. I relied on Philip Gourevitch's We Wish to Inform You for my description of the Rwandan genocide and in particular Paul Rusesabagina, whose heroism is a light in a dark period in human history. Gordon Craig's The Germans gave me the insights to describe the latent German anti-Semitism that Adolf Hitler later exploited. Gitta Sereny's Into That Darkness provided me with a chilling description of an individual who oversaw the murder of hundreds of thousands. Christopher Browning's Ordinary Men gave me a detailed account of how one German execution squad carried out its work. Loung Ung's First They Killed My Father, which I featured in the chapter on Cambodia, is a searing memoir that recounts events so terrible that they seem almost fictional. Clea Koff provided me with a firsthand account of how scientists are helping bring those who commit genocide to justice. For general research, I found the Encyclopedia of Genocide to be an invaluable resource that effectively presents and discusses an enormous range of topics on genocide.

source notes

6 Alain Destexhe, Rwanda and Genocide in the Twentieth Century (New York: New York University Press, 1995), quoted in "The Crime of Genocide," Frontline: Special Reports, 1995, http://www.pbs.org/wgbh/pages/frontline/shows/rwanda/reports/dsetexhe.html (March 2006).

8 Martin Gilbert, The Holocaust: A History of the Jews of Europe during the Second World War (New York: Henry Holt & Company, 1985), 816.

13 Peter Balakian, The Burning Tigris: The Armenian Genocide and America's Response (New York: HarperCollins, 2003), 144.

15 Samuel Totten, William S. Parsons, and Israel W. Charny, eds., Century of Genocide: Eyewitness Accounts and Critical Views (New York: Garland Publishers Inc., 1997), 71.

16 Ibid.

17 G. S. Graber, Caravans to Oblivion: The Armenian Genocide 1915 (New York: John Wiley and Sons, Inc., 1996), xii.

18 Ibid., xii–xiii.

18 Samantha Power, "A Problem from Hell": America and the Age of Genocide (New York: Basic Books, 2002), 7.

18 Graber, 153.

[19] Ibid., 154.

[19] Power, "A Problem," 13.

[20] Ibid, 15.

[21] Graber, 140.

[24] Israel W. Charny, ed. Encyclopedia of Genocide, volume 1 (Santa Barbara, CA: ABC-CLIO, 1999), 79.

[24] Power, "A Problem," 17.

[25] Ibid., 22.

[26] Bill Leadbetter, quoted in Israel W. Charny, ed., vol. 1, 272–73.

[26] Ibid., 275.

[26] Ibid.

[27] Richard Rhodes, Masters of Death: The SS Einsatzgruppen and the Invention of the Holocaust (New York: Alfred Knopf, 2002), 87.

[29] Power, "A Problem," 41–42.

[29] Ibid., 43.

[30] Charny, ed., 79.

[30] Power, "A Problem," 28.

[30] Ibid., 37.

[32] Ibid., 128.

[34] Gordon A. Craig, The Germans (New York: G. P. Putnam's Sons, Inc., 1991), 138.

[34] David Notowitz, "Voices of the Shoah, Remembrances of the Holocaust," Notowitz Productions, 2001, http://www .remember.org/carpati/VoicesSite/V oices/BookContents/VoicesTimeline .html (October 2005).

[35] Ian Kershaw, Hitler, 1889–1933: Hubris (New York: W. W. Norton & Company, Inc., 1998), 102.

[38] Saul Friedlaender, Nazi Germany and the Jews (London: Orion Publishing Co., 1997), quoted in Mitchell Bard, ed., Turning Points in History: The Holocaust (San Diego: Greenhaven Press, 2000), 54.

[38] Ibid., 55.

[40] Rhodes, 106.

[40] Christopher Browning, Ordinary Men: Reserve Police Battalion 101 and the Final Solution in Poland (New York: HarperCollins, 1992), 14.

[40] Ibid.

[41] Ibid., 2.

[41] Ibid., 63.

[41] Daniel Goldhagen, Hitler's Willing Executioners (New York: Random House, 1997), p. 22.

[42] Gilbert, 177.

[44] Browning, 27.

[45] Gitta Sereny, Into That Darkness: An Examination of Conscience (New York: Vintage Books, 1974), 158.

[47] Ibid., 122.

[47] Claude Lanzmann, Shoah: An Oral History of the Holocaust (New York: Random House, 1985), 44.

[48] Sereny, 197–8.

[48–50] Ibid., 207–8.

[51] Lanzmann, 145.

[51] Rudolf Hoess, Death Dealer: The

Memoirs of the SS Kommandant at Auschwitz, (Buffalo: Prometheus Books, 1992), 158.

[51] Ibid., 159.

[52] Elie Wiesel, Night (New York: Bantam Books, 1982), 30.

[53] Ibid., 32.

[54] Barbie Zelizer, Remembering to Forget: Holocaust Memory through the Camera's Eye (Chicago: University of Chicago Press, 1998), 84.

[58] Power, "A Problem," 50.

[58] Ibid., 51.

[59] United Nations General Assembly Resolution 96 (1), December 11, 1946, quoted in Armenian National Institute, 2005, http://www.armenian-genocide .org/Affirmation.227/current _category.6/affirmation_detail.html (May 2005).

[60] Power, "A Problem," 55.

[60] Ibid., 60.

[61] Ibid.

[64] Loung Ung, First They Killed My Father: A Daughter of Cambodia Remembers (New York: HarperCollins, 2000), 18.

[66] Power, "A Problem," 127.

[67-68] Ung, First They Killed, 58–59.

[68] Ibid., 60.

[68] Ibid.

[70] Totten, Parsons, and Charny, Century of Genocide, 340.

[70] Ung, First They Killed, 102.

[71] Ibid., 103.

[75] Power, "A Problem," 161.

[77] Philip Gourevitch, We Wish to Inform You That Tomorrow We Will Be Killed with Our Families: Stories from Rwanda (New York: Picador, 1998), 25.

[80] Fergal Keane, Season of Blood: A Rwandan Journey (London: Penguin Books, 1995), 9.

[81] Power, "A Problem," 329–30.

[81] Gourevitch, 26.

[82] Ibid., 42.

[82] Ibid., 28.

[84] Keane, Season of Blood, 78–79.

[84] Ibid., 80.

[85] Gourevitch, 24.

[86] Ibid., 116.

[86] Ibid., 127.

[87] Ibid., 128.

[88] Gourevitch, 133.

[88] Ibid.

[89] Power, "A Problem," 366.

[89] Ibid., 352.

[90] James Woods, quoted in "The Triumph of Evil" Frontline, 2005, http://www.pbs.org/wgbh/pages/ frontline/shows/evil/interviews/ gourevitch.html (September 2005).

[91] Hella Pick, "Obituary: Simon Wiesenthal," Guardian, September 21, 2005, http://www.guardian.co.uk/ obituaries/story/0,3604,1574457 ,00.html (September 2005).

[91] Ibid.

[92] James Woods, quoted in "The

Triumph of Evil."

92 Power, "*A Problem*," 383.

93 National Archives and Records Administration, "Remarks by the President to Genocide Survivors, Assistance Workers, and U.S. and Rwanda Government Officials," *Clinton Presidential Materials Project*, March 25, 1998, http://clinton6 .nara.gov/1998/03/1998-03-25 -remarks-by-the-president-to -genocide-survivors.html (May 2005).

93 Romeo Dallaire quoted in "Romeo Dallaire: Indepth," *CBC News*, October 24, 2003, http:// www.cbc.ca/news/background/ dallaire/ (May 2005).

100 Power, "*A Problem*," 277.

100 Ibid., 297.

102 Marlise Simons, "Details of Srebrenica Emerge as Hague Prepares for a Trial," *New York Times*, July 4, 2005, sec. A3.

104 Power, "*A Problem*," 405.

106 Clea Koff, *The Bone Woman: A Forensic Anthropologist's Search for Truth in the Mass Graves of Rwanda, Bosnia, Croatia, and Kosovo* (New York: Random House, 2004), 138.

108 Ibid., 153.

109 Unitd Nations, "Rome Statute of the International Court," *The United Nations*, 1998–1999, http://www .un.org/law/icc/general/overview .htm (May 2005).

110 Charny, 556.

111 Simons, sec. A3.

113 "Speech by President to the Nation," *Clinton Foundation*, March 24, 1999, http://www .clintonfoundation.org/legacy/ 032499-speech-by-president-to -the-nation.htm (June 2005).

114 "Srebrenica Report Blames UN," BBC, November 16, 1999, http:// www.news.bbc.co.uk/1/hi/world/ europe/521825.stm (May 2005).

114 Samantha Power, "Never Again— The World's Most Unfulfilled Promise," *Cambodian Genocide Group*, 2005, http://www .cambodiangenocide.org/ neveragain.htm (June 2005).

115 Gregory Stanton, "Eight Stages of Genocide," *Genocide Watch*, 1998, http://www.genocidewatch.org/ 8stages.htm (June 2005).

116 Kofi Annan, "UN Secretary- General Declares Overriding Interest of International Criminal Court Conference Must Be That of Victims and World Community as a Whole," *The United Nations* June 15, 1998, http://www.un.org/icc/ pressrel/lrom6r1.htm (September 2005).

116 Anne Applebaum, "Do We Need an International Criminal Court?" *Slate*, January 4, 2001, http://slate .msn.com/id/96110 (September 2005).

117 Ibid.

119 Fergal Keane, "Why 'Never Again' Keeps Happening," *BBC News*, July 6, 2005, http://news .bbc.co.uk/2/hi/programmes/ from_our_own_correspondent/

4641773.stm (September 2005).

122 "Annan Warns of Rwandan-Style Genocide in Sudan," *Reuters*, April 7, 2004.

123–124 Glenn Kessler and Colum Lynch, "U.S. Calls Killings in Sudan Genocide," *Washington Post*, September 10, 2004, A1.

124 Ibid.

125 Dr. Jerry Ehrlich, interview with the author, December 15, 2005.

126 Ibid.

127 Ibid.

127 Ibid.

127 Ibid.

129 Ibid.

129 Ariel Wisotsky, interview with the author, December 24, 2005.

129 Ibid.

129 Ibid.

131 "Sudan Bars Darfur Atrocity Probe," *BBC News*, December 13, 2005, http://news.bbc.co.uk/2/hi/africa/4526208.stm (December 2005).

131 "UN Warns of Fresh Darfur Threat," *BBC News*, Dec. 20, 2005, http://news.bbc.co.uk/2/hi/africa/4544116.stm (December 2005).

131 Ibid.

131 Stefan Lovgren, "'Hotel Rwanda' Portrays Hero Who Fought Genocide," *National Geographic News*, December 9, 2004, http://news.nationalgeographic.com/news/2004/12/1209_041209_hotel_rwanda.html (August 2005).

133 Viktor E. Frankl, *Man's Search for Meaning*, (New York: Simon & Schuster, 1997), 109.

134 *The Columbia World of Quotations*, as quoted on *Bartleby.com*, n.d. http://www.bartleby.com/66/29/47429.html (October 2005).

135 "Forgotten holocaust," *Guardian* (London), April 23, 2005.

135 Matthew Kaminiski, "Awaiting Trial for His Words, the Novelist Talks Turkey," *Wall Street Journal*, December 15, 2005, D8.

135–136 "Papers Across Europe on Friday Provide Vivid Coverage of Yesterday's Ceremonies at the Former Nazi Death Camp at Auschwitz on the 60th Anniversary of Its Liberation," *BBC News European Press Review*, January 1, 2005, http://news.bbc.co.uk/go/pr/fr/-/2/hi/europe/4214403.stm (January 2005).

137 "Former Khmer Rouge Leader Admits Genocide," *The Associated Press*, Dec. 30, 2003.

139 Ralph Blumenthal, "Simon Wiesenthal Is Dead at 96; Tirelessly Pursued Nazi Fugitives," *New York Times*, September 21, 2005.

139 Hella Pick, "Veteran Nazi-Hunter and Holocaust Survivor Whose Quest for Justice Set a Moral Standard for the Postwar World," *Guardian* (London), September 21, 2005.

141 John Heidenrich, *How to Prevent*

Genocide: A Guide for Policymakers, Scholars, and the Concerned Citizen (Westport, CT: Praeger Publishers, 2001), 18.

142 Jeff Otto, "Interview: Don Cheadle and Paul Rusesabagina," ign.com, December 20, 2004, http://filmforce.ign.com/articles/

574/574554p2.html (May 2005).

142 Ibid.

144 Elie Wiesel, "Nobel Prize Speech," *The Eli Wiesel Foundation for Humanity*, Dec. 10, 1986, http://www.eliewieselfoundation.org/ElieWiesel/speech.html (February 2005).

index

Page numbers in *italics* refer to illustrations.